RISE OF THE
FILMTREPRENEUR
HOW TO TURN YOUR INDEPENDENT FILM INTO A MONEYMAKING BUSINESS

BY ALEX FERRARI

Rise of the Filmtrepreneur: How to Turn Your Independent Film into a Moneymaking Business

Editor: Connie H. Deutsch
Book Design: John Garvin
Cover Art: IFH Books
Photography by: Suki Medencevic

IFH Books - A Division of IFH Industries Inc.
916-C W. Burbank Blvd #257
Burbank, CA 91506
www.ifhindustries.com

Ordering Information:
Quantity sales: Special discounts are available on quantity purchases by corporations, associations and others. For details contact the publisher at the address above.

Orders by US trade bookstores and wholesalers: Please contact the publisher at the address above.

Printed in the United States of America

Library of Congress Control Number: 1-8257004391
ISBN Paperback: 978-0-578-60865-5

First Edition

CAPRICORN
BOOK PUBLISHING

*This book is dedicated to the Indie Film Hustle Tribe
because none of this would be possible without their support.*

Keep on Hustlin'
Alex Ferrari

TABLE OF CONTENTS

Preface: Who is this Guy? IX

Chapter 1: Why Most Independent Films Fail 1

Chapter 2: What is a Filmtreprenuer? 6

Chapter 3: The Birth of the Filmtrepreneur Method 9

Chapter 4: The Vegan Chef Movie. 14

Chapter 5: The Filmtrepreneur Business Model 18

Chapter 6: The Riches are in the Niches 24

Chapter 7: Testing Your Idea 31

Chapter 8: Let's Think Outside the Box. 36

Chapter 9: Let's Make a Movie 40

Chapter 10: Finding the Money 50

Chapter 11: Building an Audience. 56

Chapter 12: Micro-Budget Filmmaking 66

Chapter 13: The Money is in the Lunchboxes 75

Chapter 14: Teach and They Will Come 84

Chapter 15: Selling Services and Yourself 92

Chapter 16: Getting Your Film into the World 96

Chapter 17: The Untold Dark Side of Film Distribution 103

Chapter 18: Video-on-Demand 112

Chapter 19: Self-Distribution 115

Chapter 20: Film Aggregators – A Warning 122

Chapter 21: Four Walling 125

Chapter 22: On-Demand Screenings 128

Chapter 23: Selling Yourself at a Film Market. 135

Chapter 24: Regional Cinema Model 138

Chapter 25: How Not to Release a Film 145

Chapter 26: Marketing 150

Chapter 27: Film Festivals. 156

Chapter 28: Test, Adjust and Pivot 165

Chapter 29: Expand and Grow 169

Chapter 30: Reversing the Filmtrepreneur Method. 175

Chapter 31: Side Hustles of the Filmtrepreneur 180

Chapter 32: Art vs Commerce. 187

Chapter 33: This is Just the Beginning. 189

Afterward: Careful What You Wish For 192

Want to Be a Filmtrepreneur? 194

Glossary of Terms 197

PREFACE

Who Is This Guy?

I would be asking the same question. My name is Alex Ferrari and I have been taking shrapnel in the film business for twenty-five years. I've worn many different hats on my filmmaking journey; production assistant, office PA, assistant editor, film editor, colorist, post-production supervisor, online editor, television promo predator, movie trailer editor, visual effects supervisor, lighting guy (though I don't consider myself a cinematographer), screenwriter, producer, and finally director. There are probably another few dozen jobs I have done while following my film-making dream but directing has always been my passion.

I've been lucky enough to work with some of the biggest companies and studios in the world and have directed music videos, commercials, television shows, streaming series, shorts and feature films. My award-winning films have been screened in close to six hundred international film festivals, sold internationally, and licensed to major streaming services like Hulu.

My first book *Shooting for the Mob* (www.shootingforthemob.com) chronicles my misadventures in Hollywood almost directing a $20 million feature film for a bi-polar ex-gangster. Yes, it's a true story. During that long chapter of my life I met billion-dollar producers, studio heads, the biggest movie stars on the planet and I even got to meet Batman. Yes, that Batman. You'll have to read that book to find out how that happened.

During my time working in post-production I had a front-row seat to hundreds of film projects. I was able to see how those films were put together, how they failed or succeeded. Working in post-production, I spent hundreds of hours in a dark room with producers and directors. I would hear stories of film production dramas and distribution nightmares.

It didn't matter if they were seasoned filmmakers or fresh out of film school they all had torturous stories they were all too happy to share. I kept seeing my fellow independent filmmakers get eaten alive by the film business and I finally had enough. In 2015, I launched *Indie Film Hustle* (www.indiefilmhustle.com) as a real and raw resource to educate and inspire filmmakers on their filmmaking path. I set out to help filmmakers with some tough love and shared whatever experience and information I had gathered on my trek through Hollyweird.

Soon after, I launched the *Indie Film Hustle Podcast*, and within three months, it became the #1 filmmaking podcast on Apple Podcasts. The show has since been downloaded millions of times by filmmakers around the world.

I have had the pleasure of interviewing hundreds of the biggest and most successful filmmakers, craftsmen, film business gurus, industry giants, million-dollar screenwriters, inspirational leaders and everyday indie filmmakers on the show.

I've always been drawn to the entrepreneurial side of the film business. As you will read in the upcoming chapters, it has been in my blood for as long as I can remember. While officially interviewing guests for my show, unofficially asking questions of filmmakers in my post-suite or working on set I began to notice patterns of success. What made one film project fly while another would come crashing down in a glowing ball of flame? I saw that the success stories would fall into three categories.

THE LOTTERY TICKET WINNERS, filmmakers being at the right place at the right time with the right product. Mythical stories like Robert Rodriguez with *El Mariachi*, Kevin Smith with *Clerks*, or Oren Peli with *Paranormal Activity* to name a few. This group went down the magical route.

THE SAVVY PRODUCER, filmmakers who understood the

marketplace and built film product based on genre, domestic and international sales, attached star power and had an understanding of budget and marketing. This group went down the traditional route.

THE OUTSIDERS, filmmakers who took a holistic approach to creating not only films, but multiple revenue streams based off those film projects. These filmmakers were outsiders making up their own rules as they went along.

I was most interested in the third group. They seemed to be more entrepreneurial in nature. I coined the word FILMTREPRENEUR to describe this group of renegades. I studied the patterns, thought processes, failures, and successes of these filmmakers. This is the subject of the book you are about to dive into.

I believe that the future of independent film will be the Filmtrepreneur Method. Independent filmmakers need to think differently. They can't play by the rules that the rest of the film industry plays by. I identified with this group so much because I was using the Filmtrepreneur Method at the beginning of my career without even knowing it but I'm getting ahead of myself.

The Filmtrepreneur is scrappy, hardworking, thinks of the business before he jumps into the show and hustles like there is no tomorrow. Before we get started, let's take a look at why most independent films fail.

CHAPTER 1

Why Most Independent Films Fail

Tell me if you heard this one before. A filmmaker, who we will call Rick, scrapes, borrows and steals money to produce his dream feature film. Rick has never actually made a feature film before but that doesn't matter; he will just hire the right people to help him realize his opus. Rick puts together a business proposal and starts hunting for money. This process takes over a year.

By some miracle Rick raises $250,000 for his film, most of which is money he got from family and friends. He even got a few investors who have always wanted to see their names on the big screen as executive producers. Rick's movie idea has been swirling in his head for years, ever since he was doodling thoughts in his notebook during math class in high school and now, finally, he will be bringing his film to life.

Rick's film is a period drama that takes place in the 90's. He decides to cast local actors and since most of the money came from family and friends he cast them in the film as well. This was one of the prerequisites for him to get the money. Oh, don't forget one of the investor's girlfriend, who just got bitten by the acting bug, wants to be in the film as well.

Let's fast-forward a bit and give Rick a best-case scenario. He was able to hire good people to work with him and shot a decent film. For the most part, the acting is acceptable and the cinematographer he hired did a good job lighting and shooting the film.

Rick is able to get the film through post-production; mind you, it took him almost another year to finish the film because he ran out of money during post. Rick spends months hustling more money to finish the film. He talks his family's dentist into ponying up the rest of the money and Rick finally finishes the film.

Now, Rick decides to submit the finished product to the Sundance Film Festival. His entire distribution plan is to get accepted to Sundance, win an award, and get a fat check from a producer or film distribution company. Then his directing career can finally take off and he can pay back his family, friends, investors, and dentist for all the support they gave him.

In 2019 the Sundance Film Festival received 12,218 submissions to its film festival. Only 118 films were selected. About 98.5% of films are rejected from the festival. When Rick receives an email telling him he didn't get into the festival he freaks out. This was his only plan, he had no backup plan. Rick has been working on this film on and off for over two years. His investors are out of patience and beginning to pressure him to get the film released.

Rick does what most filmmakers in his situation do, he starts calling random film distribution companies to see if there is anybody out there that will give him a deal. In the back of his mind, he's telling himself that everything is fine. He'll just get a big distribution company to buy his film, get a check for $300,000 and then he can pay everyone back with some interest.

Unfortunately, film distributors are not biting. Rejection after rejection comes in. Many distributors are telling him the same thing, it's extremely hard to sell a period drama with no stars attached. After a while Rick starts to reach out to more predatory film distributors because he sees no other choice. After six months of trying, one film distributor finally shows interest.

They say they can't give him any money upfront but they will do a 50%/50% revenue split. The distributor says that he travels to all the big international film markets like the American Film Market and Cannes. They believe that they can make some money overseas. They also say that they'll have his film on all the major streaming platforms within 45 days.

Rick believes his prayers have been answered. It's not exactly what he had in mind but it's better than nothing. He receives the distribution agreement and sends it over to his Uncle Bob, who is a real estate attorney, to give it a look over. Bob reads the agreement very carefully. Unfortunately, Uncle Bob doesn't know what to look for in a film distribution contract and misses all the fine print. Uncle Bob gives the go-ahead and Rick signs the contract. The length of the terms is an "industry standard" fifteen years.

True to their word the film distributor does get the film up on Apple TV, Amazon, Google Play and other VOD (Video-on-Demand) platforms. Months pass and no word from the distributor. Rick calls but it's impossible to get anyone on the phone. After a year the first revenue report comes in the mail. Rick rushes to open the letter and when he sees the numbers his mouth hits the floor. Good news, his little film has generated $20,000 in revenue from a few foreign sales to China and Germany. Amazing! The bad news, VOD sales are nonexistent. Rick told all his family and friends to buy or rent the film but not many did.

Well, $20,000 is better than nothing. As he goes to the last page of the report he's expecting to see a $10,000 check but what he finds is that the film is in the red to the tune of $30,000 plus. You see, in the contract the film distributor had to deduct film market fees, deliverable costs, travel expenses, poster design, trailer editors, graphics and a list of other expenses and, since Uncle Bob, the attorney, didn't know to look to cap these expenses this film will never see a dime in profit. This is what we in the film business call "Hollywood accounting."

So now Rick has lost control of his film, has never gotten a dime for it, can't pay back his investors, and has lost all hope of becoming a big studio director because no one will ever invest in one of his movies again after this monumental failure. Rick goes on to take a position working in a job he hates so he can make a living and gives up on his filmmaking dream. He ends up angry and bitter at the world because the film business is unfair and it didn't recognize his obvious genius.

Now, I know what you are thinking, that this is an exaggerated story and the independent film world doesn't normally work like this. Rick made a ton of mistakes and most people can't be that ignorant to the standard process of making and selling an independent film. I hate to tell you but I wish that were true. The story I just laid out is, unfortunately, all too true. Rick is a composite of many filmmaking stories I've heard or personally been a part of.

It doesn't matter if you are a seasoned professional or a film student, if you haven't gone through or educated yourself on this process you will more than likely lose money trying to sell your film. That's the problem, most filmmakers are taught that traditional distribution is the only path to making money with their independent films. Schools are teaching ideas that barely worked thirty years ago. The rules of the game have changed.

There are more opportunities for filmmakers today than ever before but with that opportunity comes more competition. Technology has made it easier than ever to produce a feature film, streaming series, or any high quality video content then ever before.

Every month thousands of feature films are dumped onto the marketplace around the world. Consumers have so much content to watch that it would take a person ten lifetimes to consume it all. Independent filmmakers have major competition for the consumer's eyeballs.

MY FILM IS GOING TO BE HUGE

I was consulting an independent filmmaker the other day and he told me that he was going to direct a romantic comedy. I asked him what the budget was and how he planned to market and sell the film. He told me that the budget would be $100,000 and he would produce the film then look for a distributor to buy it from him and get it out to the world.

I asked if he had any marquee actors attached to star in the production. "No, I just have some local actors," he said. So let's break this down, he has a romantic comedy with no marquee actors and his plan for making his money back is to pray a distribution company will pay him for the film and be responsible for all the marketing to get his film out into the world?

Mistake #1, shooting a romantic comedy is extremely broad. It is next to impossible to advertise to such a wide audience with little or no money. The Hollywood studios have the marketing budget to put ads on every billboard, bus bench, television, and iPhone in the world if they wanted to. You, as an indie filmmaker, need to think differently.

Mistake #2, $100,000 for a film with no stars and in such a broad genre is not advisable. The higher the budget goes the more recognizable the cast needs to be to attract eyeballs to your film. If a potential customer is scanning Netflix or Amazon Prime and they recognize a movie star they will be more likely to rent or stream that film.

The competition for eyeballs is fierce. It would take thousands of hours to consume all the content that is being created on a daily basis. Your small indie film is competing with studio films, amazing television, YouTube, and streaming series. In order to recoup a budget of that size, in a genre so broad, he would need star power he can't afford.

Mistake #3, if you think in today's world a distribution company is going to look at your $100,000 romantic comedy with no stars and pay you an MG or minimum guarantee, you're sorely mistaken. There's so much product in the marketplace, distribution companies have their pick of the litter. They only pay for movies that are guaranteed slam dunks.

The best way they know how to value a movie is by the movie stars attached. The more likely scenario with this film would go as follows, the distribution company would give you no money up front, offer you a horrible contract that would lock your film up for 10 to 15 years and you would probably never see a dime from any sales. This is the harsh reality of traditional distribution in today's world.

Of course, there are exceptions and outliers. This exact same movie, with the same budget, could be sold to a Lifetime Channel or Hallmark Channel but the stars would more than likely need to be television actors who would be recognized by the audiences of those channels. There are actors who have built entire careers just by starring in Lifetime and Hallmark movies. But before you call Lifetime's 800-number looking to speak to someone in the movie purchasing department, beware.

If you're an independent producer, have little or no track record and have no connection to anybody in these companies, it would be extremely difficult for you to sell your film to them. You would have to go through a traditional distribution company that has those relationships and connections.

So what chance does an indie filmmaker have in today's oversaturated marketplace? Is there any hope? What is the solution? Let's dive in.

CHAPTER 2

What is a Filmtrepreneur?

Independent filmmakers can't play the game by the same rules that everyone else is playing by. Think David and Goliath. If David would have fought the giant Goliath on his own terms, David would have never stood a chance. David fought by his own rules. The small boy picked up a rock, put it in his sling, aimed at Goliath's head, and fired. Goliath came crashing down in front of an audience of shocked soldiers from both sides.

If you try to shoot, market, and distribute, a feature film like most other independent films you will mostly fail and lose money. It is said that 98% of all independent films fail to get any kind of distribution and, fewer than that, actually recover their production budget.

The ability to manage risk and hit the bull's-eye on a film's release is extremely difficult. If you're trying to produce and market your feature film like the Hollywood studios do you will fail. You don't have the financial muscle that the studios do, nor do you have the marketing and distribution infrastructure that they have. You don't have a $100 million P&A (Prints and Advertising) budget to make everyone in the country know that your romantic comedy is coming out on Friday.

Filmtrepreneurs need to think differently, be smarter, hustle harder and play their own game. The future of independent filmmaking is going to be the entrepreneurial filmmaker or the Filmtrepreneur. The filmmaker who doesn't just understand the business side but also understands the marketing, distribution, and product development side as well. The Filmtrepreneur will understand growth hacking, viral marketing, crowdsourcing, audience building, revenue streams and alternate ways to raise money for their projects.

The Filmtrepreneur is able to pivot and change with the ever changing marketplace, adjust and exploit new technologies in film production, online marketing, and distribution methods. The Filmtrepreneur must have a command of the entire filmmaking craft, even if he doesn't perform each part of the process.

The Filmtrepreneur needs to create massive value for audiences that he can actually market and sell to. His feature films and ancillary products will be so in line with his audience's wants that they will not pay attention to the big studio blockbuster coming out on Netflix or in the theater the week of his release. In this book, I will lay out concepts and strategies as well as multiple case studies detailing successful Filmtrepreneur projects.

THE SECRET SAUCE

The secret sauce of any Filmtrepreneur is creating massive value for his or her niche audience. That value could be in the entertaining film that fulfills a need in an underserved audience or it could be in the plethora of ancillary products or services that have been spun off the feature film. Diversification in revenue streams from a given project will give a film the best chance of not only breaking even but actually making a profit. This is the secret sauce filmmakers don't understand.

So many filmmakers just want to create a film to express themselves as artists. There's absolutely nothing wrong with that but unfortunately, filmmaking is one of the most expensive art forms on the planet. If you want to create art then you need to keep the budget of your film as low as possible and be prepared to lose some if not all of your investment in the project. As film producer Suzanne Lyons says:

"There is the word SHOW and the word BUSINESS and the word BUSINESS has twice as many letters as the word SHOW."

Can you create an art film and make money with it? Of course. The Filmtrepreneur method works for any kind of film. You need to identify a niche audience, create a value-packed product (the feature film), and follow the rest of the steps I will lay out in the upcoming chapters.

As we move forward on this journey I'll be referring a lot to feature films but the Filmtrepreneur Method can also be used with streaming series, video content, YouTube channels or any other visual media.

Being a Filmtrepreneur is not all about money and business. You are working in a creative field and if you are trying to create a film or product for the marketplace then you should be enjoying the process.

If you are doing this just for the money then you will have a hard time making a go of being a Filmtrepreneur. This business is just too brutal if you don't love what you are doing day in and day out. That love will get you through the inevitable rough patches and make you soar during the monumental highs.

When the show and the business come together in a beautiful marriage, and you provide massive value to your audience, then you will have something special. Audiences are way too savvy and sophisticated nowadays. They can smell a money grab coming from a mile away. The Filmtrepreneur Method just allows you, the filmmaker, the ability to create real value for your audience and in turn generate revenue from your film without being beholden to a middleman.

You stay in control of your own destiny and you then have a fighting chance of building a business that will allow you to fulfill your dream of being a filmmaker and building an Filmtrepreneurial career.

So what is the origin of the Filmtrepreneur Method? It all started with a little short film called *BROKEN*.

CHAPTER 3

The Birth of the Filmtrepreneur Method

In 2004, I set out to direct my first serious short film as a calling card to show Hollywood that I could direct a film. My goal was to produce an extremely ambitious sci-fi action thriller. The short film was called *BROKEN*. The budget of the film was $8000 and it was shot on a Panasonic DVX100a miniDV camera, the first prosumer camera that could record video at 24 frames per second, which made the image look more filmlike. The film also boasted having over one hundred visual effects shots, an unheard-of feat for a short film in 2004.

Me lining up a shot on the set of BROKEN

With the help of my amazing cast and crew, we were able to put together one heck of a cool film. *BROKEN* went on to screen in over 200 international film festivals and was reviewed by over 150 news outlets around the world.

Even the legendary film critic Roger Ebert gave the film a positive review.

"*BROKEN* is essentially a demonstration of the mastery of horror imagery and techniques. Effective and professional. Looking forward to *BROKEN* the feature."

While I was traveling all over the country, attending film festival after film festival I kept asking the same question in my head, "How am I going to make money with this film?" No one was going to pay money to see a short film, directed by a nobody from Florida and starring unknown local actors. So how could I recoup the production costs, not to mention all the money I was spending on film festivals, submissions and travel.

BROKEN Movie Poster

I just asked one simple question, "Who is the audience for this film?" I realized that no one was going to pay just to watch this short film but a niche audience might be interested in the making of this ambitious project. That niche audience was independent filmmakers, an audience that I knew extremely well since I myself was a filmmaker and was the target audience for this new product I was about to create.

Before I jumped into the production of this new product I did market research. I studied the marketplace and realized that there was a hole that I could fill. I set out to put together a guerrilla film school, which went over every detail of the filmmaking process. From the script to production to the marketing and distribution. The total runtime would be over four hours. I authored a DVD, had it professionally mastered and replicated.

Now I had an amazing product that my niche audience, based on the market research I did, would be dying to purchase. The next question was how do I reach that audience without spending thousands of dollars on advertising?

In 2005, when *BROKEN* was released the Internet landscape was a very different place. That was the year YouTube was launched, Myspace was the dominant social media platform and message boards were all the rage. I researched where my audience was hanging out and started interacting with them there. Whether on message boards like DVXuser. com or posting on Myspace I started to get the word out on my short film and the guerrilla film school DVD.

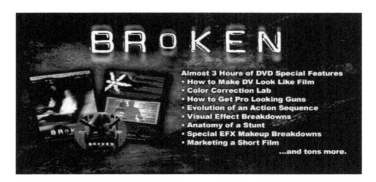

Artwork for BROKEN DVD

After months of building up the release of the DVD my niche audience was rabid for my product. Remember, there was no other product in the marketplace that filled this need. Sure there were great DVD extras from studio films but nothing that taught you how to make an independent film with off the shelf gear and software.

Release day came and I was a nervous wreck. Would anybody buy my little DVD? I had been collecting emails for months on my website from people interested in the film. I composed the announcement email to let everyone know the DVD was available and hit send.

Within minutes I started getting PayPal emails saying I had a sale. Sales kept coming and coming from customers around the world. Ding, ding, ding was the sound coming from my computer. It was crazy. I sold over 550 DVDs on that first day, that was $11,000. I recouped the budget of the film and the production costs of the DVD in one day.

Once the word got out online the sales kept coming in. In 2005 you couldn't go to a filmmaking message board on the Internet and not find my film's trailer or people not talking about the guerrilla film school on the *BROKEN* DVD. I spent weeks online investing time and building relationships with my audience.

Discussing a scene on the set of BROKEN

To this day I still run into filmmakers who mention *BROKEN* and who tell me that the DVD really helped them on their own filmmaking journey. I went on to sell over 5000 copies of *BROKEN* and if you could believe it I'm still making money with that content online through courses I developed teaching filmmakers how to make a short film.

Following the success of the short film, I launched *The Art of BROKEN* book that showcased all the amazing artwork by my collaborators Dan Cregan and Ken Robkin. Over the years I have been able to sell many copies of that book through self-publishing it on Amazon.com.

The Cover of The Art of BROKEN

Unbeknownst to me at the time, this was the origin of the Filmtrepreneur Method. Many of the techniques and methods I will discuss in this book have been tested by me over the years. I've also had the pleasure of interviewing many other Filmtrepreneurs for my *Indie Film Hustle Podcast*. I detail their successes and failures in the upcoming chapters. Let's put these ideas to the test. Anyone interested in vegan food tonight?

CHAPTER 4

The Vegan Chef Movie

Now let's look at our filmmaker Rick's scenario again, but this time let's tackle it using the Filmtrepreneur Method. First, I would try to find out what could be the lowest budget, while still maintaining great production value. You have to think like a lean start-up, keep your overhead low. The lower the budget the easier it will be to recoup and profit from your film.

Next I would just tweak the idea a bit. Making a romantic comedy is fine but you have to niche down. Instead of trying to make a film that is targeted to the masses, the key is to make a product that you, yourself, could market to a niche audience.

Why not make this a film about a vegan chef who falls in love with a barbecue champion. We'll call this movie *Crazy, Sexy, Vegan*. You have built-in conflict and all types of scenarios for romance and comedy. Now changing this to a vegan chef movie allows you, as the Filmtrepreneur, to market the film to multiple niche audiences that you could actually reach.

With targeted ads on *Facebook* and *Google* you can target vegans, vegetarians, people interested in healthy living and a plant-based diet, fitness enthusiasts, yoga, and multiple other sub-niches. You can also target people who liked some popular plant-based diet documentaries like *Forks Over Knives* or *Food Matters*. These are just a few marketing methods you could use to reach your new niche audience.

Now that you have a smaller audience to target let's see what ancillary products we can create to accompany this film. If I was making a vegan chef movie I would look to partner with a vegan chef, maybe even a celebrity vegan chef who has an online social media following. That vegan chef could not only guest star in the film but wouldn't it make sense if that chef creates a series of online courses teaching people how to make vegan dishes that are spotlighted in the film? You can partner with the chef on these courses. It's a win-win for both of you.

You could even include building online courses into the story line of the film. The vegan chef is broke and his new barbecue champion, meat-eating girlfriend is also an online marketing specialist by day and helps him launch a new business. I'm just spitballing here.

If you are a vegan customer interested and watching a romantic comedy about a vegan chef who falls in love with a meat-eater is it possible that the same customer would be interested in purchasing courses about veganism, plant-based cookbooks, and vegan merchandise like t-shirts, hats, and aprons?

Wouldn't it also make sense to reach out to companies that sell vegan products and see if they would be interested in product placement inside your film? How about teaming up with organizations that promote veganism, plant-based diets, animal rights, and healthy lifestyles? Considering that there aren't many vegan chef movies in the world it might be a great opportunity for you and these companies and organizations.

You can make deals with these companies for free products for the film or for actual cash that can go toward your final budget. You can also make these companies your media partners. These companies have large email lists and social media followings of customers who love their vegan products.

Do you think that these customers would be interested in your film and ancillary products? By partnering with these companies you might not even have to spend much money on actual marketing. You can direct market to customers who would be interested in your film and products.

The regular filmmaker would just try to take this finished film to a traditional film distributor in hopes that they would either pay him a decent MG (Minimum Guarantee) or at least give him a deal so the distributor would then try to sell the film for him. As I illustrated in my prior story this would not be very wise for a film like this. The Filmtrepreneur has to think differently.

The Filmtrepreneur would look for alternate ways to release the film to the niche audience he is targeting. Here are a few examples, which I will explain in upcoming chapters. You could four wall a movie theater yourself locally where your vegan chef partner lives.

Hopefully she would have been promoting the film to her customers via her restaurant. Then you might be able to take the show on the road to large cities that have big vegan and vegetarian populations. After months of cultivating an online audience you should be able to put out feelers to see what cities would be interested in hosting a screening. You would be able to target those people using Facebook and Google ads via location tracking.

After your theatrical run you could upload your film to a site like *Vimeo* where you could sell not only your film but your series of online vegan chef courses as a package. You could also add exclusive interviews on how to become vegan and transition to a more plant-based diet.

You can also launch your online courses separately and leverage the film in the marketing. Uploading your courses onto multiple online learning platforms will generate passive income and serve as marketing materials for your film and the new vegan/plant-based diet eco-system you are creating.

Now you have multiple revenue streams generating revenue everyday. You are making money while you sleep. After about three months you launch the film on the more traditional platforms using an aggregator or by partnering with a traditional distributor to upload your film to Apple TV, Amazon and Google for TVOD (Transaction-Video-On-Demand). You drive traffic to those platforms and customers who have been waiting for your film to come on their favorite streaming platform will finally buy the film and be introduced to your eco-system.

Next up merchandise. Your passionate niche audience wants t-shirts, hats, and aprons based on the movie. You also create a line of clothing based around being or becoming a vegan.

Based on the popularity of the film and courses you start to develop multiple series of online courses and original content. Your audience has grown so much that you decide to launch your own OTT (Streaming Service/Membership Site) where you create original content monthly for your members. After a while you put the film up on Amazon Prime for free through their SVOD (Subscription-Video-On-Demand) as a loss leader to get your brand's name out there even more, while still generating additional revenue from the platform.

As a result of all the revenue and awareness for *Crazy, Sexy, Vegan* you decide to leverage that success and dive into shooting a documentary about plant-based eating. Since you already cultivated a very passionate audience it will be much easier to sell this new feature documentary to them.

Then you start this entire process again with your new film but you can now leverage your existing niche audience. You could even make the digital world premiere on your streaming service since the monthly memberships more than pay for the budget of the film. You've become a mini-Netflix for your niche audience.

Do you think this scenario is a bit far-fetched? Every single idea I just laid out has been executed by me or other Filmtrepreneurs in the world. It is not only possible, but this is the type of thinking you will need to use to thrive in the independent film business moving forward.

The Filmtrepreneur thinks of a feature film as just one part of a larger business plan. In many ways the feature film is just the marketing tool to sell ancillary products and services.

As we continue on our Filmtrepreneur journey we will be discussing alternative ways of generating revenue from an independent feature film. Many of the ideas you are about to read are outside of the Hollywood box. With this book I'm attempting to change the way filmmakers look at making independent films. I'm trying to start a movement.

The old model is outdated and doesn't work anymore. There's too much competition for attention in the world today and the film industry is changing so fast that if you don't adapt the business will run right over you.

I wanted to share this fictional case study to illustrate what is possible with a feature film using the Filmtrepreneur Method. So let's breakdown what the Filmtrepreneur Method is.

CHAPTER 5

The Filmtrepreneur Business Model

A Filmtrepreneur approaches the making of a feature film in a holistic way. The film can be the main revenue generator but there should always be other products and/or services that generate recurring revenue as well. The old model of production and distributing independent film is obsolete for most filmmakers working today. Sure, there will always be outliers, but the rest of us must learn how to increase the odds in our favor. I believe the Filmtrepreneur Method does just that. Below I have listed the main categories of the Filmtrepreneur Method. In the upcoming chapters I will go into greater depth of each of these areas.

IDENTIFY YOUR NICHE

Before you go down the path of developing, writing, producing and selling a feature film you need to understand who you are creating the film for. Understanding your audience and what they want is imperative. You should identify a niche audience first then create a film and product lines for that audience.

Filmmakers should back into the story based on the audience they are trying to target. Many indie filmmakers will write a screenplay and then look for the locations, props and people to fit their story. The Filmtrepreneur needs to think differently.

When you "back into" the writing of a story it means you take inventory of the resources you have and write your screenplay around those things. If you have access to your friends Tesla, an Italian restaurant and three police costumes left over from a Halloween party then you should write those resources into your story. By using the "backing in" method you add much more production value into your movie.

Hollywood studios can write whatever they want into their movies because they have almost unlimited resources to bring their projects to life. Generally indie filmmakers have more challenging filmmaking budgets. Famed film director Robert Rodriguez pioneered this method with his first film *El Mariachi*. He had relationships with the leaders of a small Mexican town, access to the local police station, an arsenal of guns, a dog, a turtle, his lead actor and a guitar case. He wrote all those resources into his film and packed in a tremendous amount of production value into his humble $7000 feature film.

MARKET RESEARCH

Once you have a few potential niche audiences on your list then you should begin doing market research on the group of potential customers. Does your niche audience want or need to see this film? Can the potential audience support the budget of the film project? Will the project have a good ROI (Return on Investment) and ROT (Return on Time)? Would the niche be likely to purchase ancillary products from the film? Is the niche audience too broad for you to penetrate with your marketing efforts or too small to support your project at all?

REVENUE STREAMS RESEARCH

Now that you've chosen a niche audience, what products or services would they be likely to purchase? Could you sell a service to them? Is there potential for affiliate sales? What are the hard costs of the physical and/or digital products?

FILM PROJECT DEVELOPMENT

So, you have a niche. You have solid ideas for a potential product, revenue streams and you have started interacting with your niche; now you need to develop the feature film. During this stage you will be brainstorming ideas, writing screenplays or scriptments and thinking about all the moving parts that go into producing your film. Don't let the "to do" list intimidate you but I would suggest making a checklist of all the things that have to go into producing your project.

The first thing that you should nail down is doing the math to determine what the budget will be. Be realistic about how much money you can lay your hands on, keeping in mind that, like any other business, there may be hidden costs that could prevent you from bringing your film to fruition. Once you're sure of your financing, then you can turn your attention to locations, equipment needs, what resources you could use in the film and who you can enlist to help you bring the film to life.

After you have locked down the film script or scriptment, more on scriptments later, you should register the copyright of the film project with the Library of Congress. This protects you, your project and your business. You will need to register the script and then the final film once it is completed. If you believe you have a unique film property, you should also trademark the name of the film for use in selling ancillary products or services. Creating a trademark protects your IP or intellectual property. If George Lucas hadn't trademarked *Star Wars* then anybody could slap the *Star Wars* logo on a t-shirt and sell it. Just something to keep in mind.

FINANCING

Every filmmaker's favorite part of the process, finding money. Of course, I'm being sarcastic. At this stage you will have few options like crowdfunding, finding outside investors or funding the film project yourself. You will also need to think about any costs related to physical or digital products you will be creating for this film. Don't forget to put aside money for marketing as well.

AUDIENCE BUILDING

At this stage, you should begin engaging your niche audience online. Where does your niche hang out online? What events or conventions does your niche attend? What organizations does your audience belong to? Observe and interact with them. Provide value to them at the start. Do not, I repeat, do not make any requests or try to sell anything at this stage. You are building a relationship. You need to be of service to the audience. At the same time, you will need to begin the process of building your own online audience.

ANCILLARY PRODUCT DEVELOPMENT

While the feature film is being developed you should be thinking of ancillary products and passive income streams that could be sold from the film or IP (intellectual property). Some products will be inspired by the film and others could be placed in the film during production. Thinking this way opens you up to more revenue opportunities.

You should also be planning who your behind the scenes production team will be. What footage will you need for the product lines you plan to create? For me on BROKEN, the behind the scenes was just as important as the main production because the guerrilla film school I developed from that footage was the driving force of all my DVD and online sales.

PRODUCTION

Let's make a movie. At this stage, you are in production of your feature film. Have fun, enjoy the process and make sure you get everything you need for both the film and the ancillary products.

ANCILLARY PRODUCT PRODUCTION

You are finally done with the principal production of your film. Rest for a weekend and back to work on Monday. You now jump into the long process of post-production where you put together your final product. The production team has captured your raw material and now it's time to build a product that your niche audience will love and purchase. This is the perfect time to begin building your ancillary product lines, behind the scenes, documentaries, digital and physical products, and passive income streams. You want everything ready when you launch your film.

FILM DISTRIBUTION PLAN

Your feature film is done. Now you need to think about how you will be releasing your baby to the world. Will you start with film festivals or go straight to traditional distributors? Are you going to self-distribute? Does it make sense to work with a film aggregator? Will you do it on your own and just upload it to Amazon Prime yourself? Each film has its own path to walk; it's your job to discover what the path is and then optimize it as much as possible.

ANCILLARY PRODUCT DISTRIBUTION PLAN

The film is in the pipeline to get distributed. Do you have a plan to distribute your digital or physical products? Do you have systems in place to ship physical products or will you be using a drop shipping company? Will you purchase large batches of the product upfront or produce products as your customer orders them? These systems need to be in place before you launch.

MARKETING

The great equalizer. Will you be using guerrilla marketing, grass roots, growth hacking, Facebook ads, YouTube/Google ads, or will you go the more traditional route like billboards and bus stops? Will you purchase a booth at your niches' conventions or sponsor a podcast? Do you have any money allocated for marketing? Are you doing this yourself or hiring an outside consultant? If you don't have a clear marketing plan at this stage, everything you've done to this point will be for nothing.

ANALYTICS AND METRICS

Once the marketing machine is up and running you need to be able to analyze the metrics of what your ads and energy are doing. What are your ROI and ROT? Are you A/B testing ads? Which methods are bringing in a better return on investment?

PIVOT AND ADJUST

Once those metrics come back you should be constantly pivoting and adjusting your campaigns until you find the sweet spot. At this moment, if your ROI is greater than the money you are putting in, then you need to feed that marketing beast.

EXPAND AND GROW

Depending on the ROI of the project you could either continue promoting existing product lines or you can develop new ones depending on if the market is willing. At this point, many Filmtrepreneur projects see the end of the line. The film has been released and the products have sold but the sales have slowed or stopped and you have reached mass saturation of your niche. Other Filmtrepreneurs will see even more opportunities and begin to build an evergreen brand or company around the film or series of films.

RINSE AND REPEAT

If you can do it once you can do it again. After you have mastered the Filmtrepreneur Method you'll have the option to duplicate it with every film project you do. Some films will launch a company, a series of films and products. Other films will live through their lifecycles and come to an end. If you create the system correctly you could make residual income from both scenarios for many years to come and, might I dare to say, make a sustainable business out of your art. This is the Filmtrepreneur Method. It's hard work but once you put the effort in at the beginning of this process you can continue to reap the rewards for years to come. I'm still making money every day from a short film I made fourteen years ago. It does work. Let's jump into finding a niche audience for your feature film.

CHAPTER 6

The Riches are in the Niches

Many filmmakers make the mistake of trying to reach a broad audience with their indie films. They follow the model that has been established by the Hollywood studios for decades. The problem is that you, as an independent filmmaker, do not have the budget or marketing muscle to reach every man, woman, and child in the country. This is why most independent films fail.

I know what you are thinking, "What about those success stories of filmmakers making an indie film on their iPhone, getting into Sundance and getting offered a Marvel Studios movie to direct?" Those are the exceptions, not the rule. I call those stories "Lottery Ticket Winners."

Does someone, somewhere in the world, win a lottery of millions of dollars every week? Yes. Do millions if not billions of other people lose every week as well? Yes. Having a lottery ticket mentality with your independent film is the fastest way for you to run into trouble.

Where filmmakers need to focus, is on the niche audience. A niche is a smaller segment of the general population. Let's take for example the millions of comic book fans in the world. They are a niche and a smaller segment of the population. Unfortunately, this is where many filmmakers stop.

They say to themselves I'm going to create a film for this huge niche like comic book fans, science fiction fans or people who love romance novels. The niche might be a smaller segment of the general population but it is still massive. You, as an independent filmmaker, would not be able to market to every comic book fan in the niche.

You have to niche down. Keep digging in that huge niche until you find that nugget of gold. Within the niche of comic book fans, there are hundreds of sub-niches like Marvel fans, DC Comic fans, fans of independent comics, Japanese anime fans, MCU (Marvel Cinematic Universe) fans, people who love to dress up in cosplay (when fans dress up as a specific fictional or real-life character, usually at conventions or events) and too many more to name here. Within each of those sub-niches, there are even more niches.

But be careful not to niche down too far. For example, if you pick a niche like people who love Moon Knight, an obscure Marvel superhero, and you try to make a film targeting this niche you will probably not do well. This niche is too specific and can't support a Filmtrepreneur business model of a film, ancillary products, and services. It's a balancing act that you will need to master.

In the book, *Blue Ocean Strategy: How to Create Uncontested Market Space and Make the Competition Irrelevant* by W. Chan Kim and Renée Mauborgne, the authors discuss a revolutionary market research method. If you are about to take a product to market you have a choice of what market you want to try to compete in, a blue ocean or a red ocean.

The analogy goes like this, if you want to go fishing you want to go where the fishing is easy, the problem is, so does everyone else. Where everyone knows there are tons of fish. The competition will be fierce so there will be blood in the water, a red ocean.

In the indie filmmaking world if you make an independent action film, with unknown actors, no marketing budget and try to compete with one of the major studios' blockbuster films you will be eaten alive and blood will most definitely be in the water. Not only is there too much competition in those waters but industry giants fish there as well.

Now let's say you journey out into an uncharted part of the ocean, waters there haven't been fished in yet. Your research shows that there is a good amount of fish swimming around in this part of the ocean. There aren't as many fish as in the red ocean but more than enough to feed your village and since there is no competition the fishing will be easy.

No competition, no blood in the water, a blue ocean.

– CASE STUDY –

The Resurrection of Jake the Snake

Whether he knew it or not, when Steve Yu, the filmmaker behind the documentary *The Resurrection of Jake The Snake*, released his film he was fishing in a blue ocean. The film follows the rise, fall and resurrection of legendary WWF (World Wrestling Federation) professional wrestling star Jake the Snake Roberts.

It was a heart-wrenching film that answered the question that many WWF fans had, "Whatever happened to Jake the Snake Roberts?" The film was positioned perfectly. It was a product that the niche audience of the old-school WWF and wrestling fans didn't even know they wanted.

At the time of the release there was very little, if any competition in the marketplace for a film like this, spotlighting older wrestlers that the niche audience grew up with. This film wasn't targeting a mass audience, they were trying to create a feature film that the niche they felt they could reach, would purchase and enjoy.

Even though the filmmakers received multiple distribution offers after their world premiere Slamdance Film Festival screening, they decided to think more like a Filmtrepreneur and take control of their own destiny. They opted to self-distribute their film and went through a film aggregator, which allowed them to put their film on the major TVOD streaming platforms.

On their launch day *The Resurrection of Jake The Snake* rocketed to the top of the iTunes charts and was the #1 documentary on iTunes and in the top 25 of all the titles on the platform. That is the power of a niche audience that you provide massive value to.

Once you decide on a niche you need to ask yourself what is the potential ROI for the project. Every Filmtrepreneur should ask the following questions before they set out to create an independent film for a niche audience.

WHAT IS THE SIZE OF THE NICHE?

You need to analyze the size of the niche you have chosen. Yes it may be smaller than the general population but do you have a fighting chance of actually reaching this audience?

CAN I REACH THIS NICHE AUDIENCE?

You might feel that you can reach a segment of that niche audience but will that be enough to recoup the time and money you will be putting into your film project? Understand whether you can reach the niche through paid advertising or free viral methods will determine if you have a successful or disastrous film release.

WHAT BUDGET DOES THIS NICHE AUDIENCE JUSTIFY?

This is the tricky part. You find a niche and feel that you can market your film to that niche but then you spend $500,000 on a film. That niche audience cannot support a budget that high. Are there enough people in that niche who are willing to not only purchase or rent your film but might also be willing to purchase some of your ancillary products and spread the word about your film?

Let's say you want to make a niche film about Marvel Comics cosplayers who battle DC Comics cosplayers every month in a tournament, does this cosplay niche justify a $500,000 budget film? The budget might be too expensive to be supported by that niche. You would have to incorporate other elements in that film to appeal to a larger segment of the comic book fans niche or cast bigger name actors to justify the budget.

This is why Hollywood blockbusters are so safe and sanitized. If a studio is risking $400 million dollars on a film, they can't concentrate in niches, they need to appeal to the broadest audience possible to not only recoup their investment but be profitable. This is why seeing big Hollywood studios producing risky or experimental films is extremely rare.

HOW MANY UNITS DO I NEED TO SELL?

Here's some basic math, if my film costs $50,000, then I need to sell 5000 copies at $10 each to break even. You can rent 10,000 units at $5 or a combination of both. This could either be through public theatrical screenings, streaming on Apple TV or Amazon, physically selling DVDs, Blu-Rays, SVOD, TVOD or AVOD. You'll also have to include costs of working with a film aggregator to put your films on those streaming platforms, producing physical media, rental of a theater or space for public screenings and the cost of film deliverables to submit to SVOD or AVOD platforms.

DOES THE FILM HAVE THE POTENTIAL TO BREAK OUT FROM ITS CORE NICHE?

What's even better than having a film project that targets a niche audience is a film project that breaks out and finds an audience that was never intended. That is exactly what happened when *Napoleon Dynamite* was released to the world. The film was an obscure independent film with unknown actors and a budget of $400,000. The film seemed to be positioned as a quirky indie film aimed at a small portion of the population. It wasn't particularly well received by critics and only had an opening of $144,000.

The filmmakers never in their wildest dreams expected the film to become a pop culture phenomenon. *Napoleon Dynamite* went on to gross over $44 million and continued to play in theaters for 9 months (according to BoxOfficeMojo.com). The cornucopia of merchandise from the film is mind boggling. Every once in a while you can still see people wearing a "Vote for Pedro" t-shirt. It's difficult, if not impossible, to predict a breakout hit film but you can investigate to see if there is any potential for the film to appeal to other audiences and not just to your niche.

HOW DOES THIS NICHE CONSUME FILMS?

Many filmmakers produce their film and put it out to the world using the distribution methods that everyone else uses not thinking about how their audience consumes content? A Filmtrepreneur uses a sniper rifle and not a shotgun approach to the entire process of making, marketing and selling of the film. They need to think more strategically and optimize the distribution pipeline to produce the maximum return on investment.

If you are aiming at a younger YouTube-based niche audience, then DVDs don't make sense since most of that audience is used to streaming their content. If you are targeting horror fans then DVD, Blu-Rays and even VHS tapes should be part of your distribution plan, as that audience loves physical media. Understanding the answer to this question can save you time and money and can generate more sales.

WHAT POTENTIAL PRODUCTS CAN I CREATE FOR THIS AUDIENCE?

Start thinking what ancillary products your niche audience would be interested in. If you are making that vegan chef movie then online courses and cookbooks teaching vegan meals might work very well.

If you are making a 1980's style slasher horror film then a special edition VHS package that includes a t-shirt, hat and a bloody toy axe all packed into an old school metal lunchbox might be perfect for that niche audience. How about if you direct an indie film about superheroes, then maybe a special edition comic book and statue could work well.

It doesn't have to always be physical products. You can sell services, or work as an affiliate to other products that your audience might be interested in. I discuss affiliate marketing in-depth in chapter 31.

ARE THERE ACTORS OR TALENT YOU CAN CAST SPECIFIC TO THE NICHE?

Thinking outside the box is crucial as a Filmtrepreneur. When casting your film, are there actors or celebrities of that niche who could be in your film? Often actors or celebrities who are big in a niche are infinitely more affordable than mainstream movie stars and actually mean more to that niche audience.

Take the horror niche. Let's say there's an actor who played the maniacal serial killer in a series of famous horror films, that actor has very little mainstream star power anymore unless he's playing the legendary character he brought to life all those years ago.

But that actor has much more ROI or value to the horror niche audience. Putting that actor in your film automatically taps into his core fans and easily grabs the attention of other potential customers in the horror niche. In that niche, he's a bigger movie star than Brad Pitt or Dwayne "The Rock" Johnson. You could also pepper your entire film with lesser known actors with "street credibility" in the horror niche.

Just asking these series of questions could save you hundreds if not thousands of dollars and years of your life. The answers can help you determine whether to start down the long road of making an independent film or to pull back, reassess, and change direction.

START WHERE YOU KNOW

When screenwriters first start writing, the advice they hear the most is "Write what you know." I couldn't agree more. I'm a huge proponent of going after the lowest hanging fruit first. This is exactly what I did with my film *BROKEN*. I created products that were targeted to a niche I knew better than most filmmakers. I suggest you do the same. What niche are you already a member of?

If you are a horror fan, then making a horror film might be the way to go. You know what your niche audience wants because you are a part of that niche. You become the customer for the product you are trying to create.

If you were you a wrestler in high school and college maybe you should make the wrestling movie that you always wanted to see. You already have a ton of market research inside your head because of your life experience. You would have a major head start over me if I would try to create a film about wrestling. I would make a film based on my limited experience of watching wrestling movies and my short tenure as a high school wrestler in gym class.

If you are a dancer, maybe make a film about your style of dance. If you are a skateboarder or surfer then make films about those niches. You know the audience because you are the audience. Use every advantage that you can in this process. The answers you are searching for might be right under your nose. Now let's see if your film idea is going to work.

CHAPTER 7

Testing Your Idea

You have now identified a niche audience that you believe you can create massive value for. The niche isn't too crowded for your idea and the competition is minimal if any at all. Now it's time to do some market research to see if your idea will pass the test.

Many filmmakers make the mistake of starting with creating a film project first and then think about who they can sell it to. The problem is that using this method generates an extreme amount of risk to the capital and time you invested in said film. Do you think Apple just releases a new product to the marketplace without doing an insane amount of research? Filmtrepreneurs need to think about minimizing risk as much as possible.

When you don't have deep pockets you can't take the chances that the studios do and even then they minimize risk as much as possible. Occasionally studios still release films like *John Carter from Mars*, which had a total reported cost of $350+ million and a production budget of $263 million. It was easily one of the most expensive films ever made and the film only grossed $73 million in the domestic box office. Even the "professionals" in Hollywood get it wrong sometimes.

Now imagine you are investing your mom and dad's retirement money in your feature film, do you think it would be a good idea to see if the marketplace wants to see your creation?

WHERE IS YOUR AUDIENCE?

There are many ways that you can see if your idea has any merit. You first need to identify where your niche is spending time. Some of the methods fall into two categories, passive research and active research. Passive research is when you investigate areas that don't require you to interact with the audience. Methods like Google, Quora and Medium.

And, obviously, active research is the opposite, where you do engage with the audience by using methods like Facebook Groups, Subreddits and message boards. With that said, you can use any or all of the methods to see if your idea will fly.

QUICK RESEARCH

One quick way to see if you even have a viable audience for your product is to see how many people are in your niche's groups, message boards or subreddits. If you do a search on Facebook for a niche audience on basket weavers and one group comes up with one hundred and fifty two people in it that is a sign that you probably don't have a niche large enough to support the basket weaving epic film you were planning to do. Let me introduce you to a few platforms where you can do deep market research.

FACEBOOK GROUPS

Groups have become extremely popular on Facebook. The power of these groups is that thousands if not tens of thousands, of people who are interested in a certain niche, hang out and discuss their love. You can easily join most of these groups without any issues. Most of the time there are multiple groups dedicated to your desired niche.

Once you join a group, start to comment on other members' posts. After you have spent time engaging with the members then you can begin to ask questions to gauge their interest in your potential film. I can't tell you how powerful of a tool this is.

SUBREDDITS

If you ever used the Internet then you have probably heard of Reddit. Reddit calls itself the "front page of the Internet," and it's not just marketing. According to Alexa.com the site is the 18th most visited site in the world. Reddit is a massive collection of forums where users can share stories, content from around the web, and make comments on other users' posts.

Subreddits are subset categories or forums within the Reddit website. Here is where you will find your niches. Reddit users are infamously territorial of their subreddits so if they feel you are there just to milk the forum for information they will come out guns a blaring. Best plan of action is to engage and honestly be of value and service to the community, which will also help you to build up a good Karma account.

Reddit Karma is a scoreboard for a user's account. The website uses upvotes or downvotes as its point system. You gain points when your comments or posts are upvoted and you equally lose points when they are downvoted. The higher the karma score the best reputation you have on Reddit.

You don't have to engage but to get the most out of Reddit you should try to join the party. You could also just watch and read what other users are posting and saying. I've fallen down a Subreddit rabbit hole too many times to mention.

MESSAGE BOARDS

In the world of - groups and subreddits you might think that no one is using old-fashioned message boards anymore, but you would be sorely mistaken. When I was thinking of putting together the guerrilla film school for my short film *BROKEN*, it was the message boards that gave me my best market research.

Message board users are also extremely passionate. Once you have built a rapport with the community it can become a treasure trove of feedback for your project.

TWITTER HASHTAGS

According to the dictionary, the definition of a hashtag is *a word or phrase preceded by a hash sign (#), used on social media websites and applications, especially Twitter, to identify messages on a specific topic.*

Using hashtags on twitter is a great way to jump into the conversation of your specific niche. Your job as a Filmtrepreneur is to eventually insert your film project into your niche's conversations. If you type into Twitter #vegan or #surfer you will see what people are saying regarding those niches in real time. You can use hashtags on any platform that used them like YouTube, Facebook, Instagram, and Snapchat.

GOOGLE

Google is a great resource. Simply searching for keywords associated with your target audience and seeing what Google thinks, is a great way to see what people and websites are writing about your niche.

Also, checking how many search results come up from a key term will help you gauge your potential audience's interest. You can find the number of search results in the top left area of Google after you do a search.

QUORA

Quora is a question-and-answer website where users ask and answer questions for each other. The answers are edited by users in the form of opinions. If you have a question Quora probably has the answer. If you want almost instant feedback then go on Quora, search for your niche and ask a question. People will give you opinions quickly.

MEDIUM

Created by Evan Williams, the co-founder of Twitter and Blogger.com, Medium is a platform where people can read and post articles. Doing a search in your niche would give you instant insight on what people are thinking and saying in your target niche. If there's controversy in your niche you will find an article about it here.

Medium is also a great place to discover story ideas for your film project. I would not only follow and read other people's work: if you decide to move forward with your project, posting original articles about your niche is a great way to establish yourself as a thought leader in your niche.

IT'S ALL IN THE TITLE

When doing research you should be testing different titles for your film.

Is there some word or phrase that your niche audience would recognize instantly? In the skateboarding niche, The Z-Boys are pioneers of skateboarding as we know it today. A documentary called *Dogtown and the Z-Boys* hits that niche perfectly. The audience knew exactly what that film was about and rushed out to see the film.

If they would have called the same movie *"Skateboarding Legends"* it would not have resonated as much with the core niche audience they were targeting. Keep that in mind when naming your film.

BECOMING A THOUGHT LEADER

A thought leader is someone who people, within a certain niche, follow because of the time and energy they give to the community. When Pat Flynn from Smartpassiveincome.com launched his website and podcast, his goal was to become a thought leader in the online marketing space. Author, speaker, and serial entrepreneur, Gary Vanderchuk, has built a multimillion dollar empire based on his hustle and being a thought leader in the entrepreneurial space.

When you create massive value and are truly serving a community, you become a thought leader almost by default. The more time and care you put into a community the more that group will look to see what you are doing within the community. You don't need to be a thought leader in a niche if you want to be a Filmtrepreneur but it can definitely be valuable to your endeavors.

CHAPTER 8

Let's Think Outside the Box

The cornerstone of the entire Filmtrepreneur Method is thinking of your independent film as a business with multiple products and revenue streams. This one mindset will change how you make films moving forward. So, let's think outside the box.

You have already found a niche audience that cannot only support your filmmaking ambitions but also has great potential for purchasing other products or services. Now we need to see what revenue streams can be created from your film and niche. First, you need to analyze your film and ask the following questions.

- What products does my niche audience have a history of purchasing?
- What products can be created from my indie film?
- What possible service would my niche audience be interested in?
- Is there an underserved need that I could fulfill for my niche audience?
- How can I provide free value to my niche audience?

Let's tackle each question one at a time.

What products does my niche audience have a history of purchasing?
When you are studying a niche you should see what product lines they

have a history of purchasing. If you are making that classic 80's style slasher horror film then that niche has a history of purchasing VHS Collector's Edition versions of the films they love. A bonus in that example is that there's very little competition.

Not many filmmakers are taking the time to handcraft VHS collectors' editions. So when that niche audience sees a unique product like a VHS of a new film they jump on it. If you do a little research you'll find that there is a rabid fan base for VHS tapes in the world. You can also crossover and tap into that niche audience as well. The horror niche has some of the most passionate collectors anywhere.

What products can be created from my indie film?
Once you have an understanding of what products your niche audience is buying or wants to buy then you need to begin creating unique product lines. The standard t-shirts and hats is what many filmmakers already do. There's nothing wrong with that but know that you're competing with all t-shirts and hat sellers in the world. You have to have a unique value proposition for someone to purchase a t-shirt or hat of an indie film.

Let's say that you have produced a film about ballet dancers. What products do ballet dancers use? Tote bags, ballet shoes, tape for their shoes, leg warmers? You could brand your film on these items. If the customer loves your film they might be more inclined to purchase these unique products.

If the title of your film is really inline with your niche they might just purchase your products based on that and never even watch your film. Do the research and you'll be amazed at what product ideas you can come up with. The more targeted the products are, the better.

What possible service would my niche audience be interested in?
Let's say you direct a documentary on film editing software. This might not be a riveting topic for the general public but it could be a gold mine to the niche audience of motion picture editors and filmmakers.

If you are a film editor could you sell your editing services to that audience? Let's say you've been working in post-production for years and you have taken multiple indie films all the way through the end of the post-production process, overseeing the entire post-process workflow, could you sell your services as a post-production specialist, editor or colorist? You can achieve this in two ways.

1. Self-Product Placement: You can place yourself in the documentary discussing your experiences in your field. By doing this you set yourself up as an industry thought leader and people are more likely to hire you based on your perceived experience and skill level.

2. The Calling Card Technique: By creating this documentary you have created an amazing calling card showcasing your talents and skills. Whether it's writing, directing, post-production, visual effects, or consulting, I've known many filmmakers who have gotten job offers after their films have been released.

When I released my short film *BROKEN* I was getting a few calls a week from filmmakers wanting me to color grade and post-supervise their films. Some even asked me to consult on marketing and distribution. There were so many offers I opened a post-production company to be able to field the potential clients.

Is there an underserved need that I could fill for my niche audience?
Again I'll use the example of the guerrilla film school I created for my short film *BROKEN*. In 2005 there was no online education about the filmmaking process, let alone about the indie filmmaking process. I saw my niche audience was being underserved and I filled that need with my product.

How can I provide free value to my niche audience?
A great way to attract attention from a niche audience is to create free resources and content for them to consume. Adding value and being of service to an audience is a powerful way to make a connection.

WHAT IS OLD IS NOW NEW AGAIN

I just want to address the powerful concept of nostalgia. As the world continues to grow and change at a bullet's pace many people long for the "good old days" of their youth or of perceived better times.

Hollywood has been tapping into nostalgia for years as the never-ending parade of film and television reboots can attest to. The way that the creators behind Netflix's breakout hit, *Stranger Things*, uses nostalgia, is a masterclass that all Filmtrepreneurs should study.

By tapping into 80's pop culture, films, music and art, *Stranger Things* became Netflix's number one original series. Even the *Stranger Things* logo was taken from legendary author's Stephen King's horror novel artwork he released during that time. It's subtle but when you first see the Stranger Things logo it seems familiar for some reason. The show was brilliantly executed and it also helps that the series is wonderfully written and directed.

The filmmakers even peppered the cast with 80's era movie stars to make your trip down memory lane complete. When Netflix released the first season on DVD and Blu-Ray, the artwork for the box looked like an old and weather-beaten VHS case. They knew exactly how to market to their niche audience, fans of the 80's, which is a monstrous niche.

Netflix has the budget and marketing muscle to reach that size audience. If an independent filmmaker would try to do the same thing they would have to niche down to a smaller segment of that niche. In chapter 13 we will break down how writer/director Drew Marvick was able to do just that with his independent horror slasher film *Pool Party Massacre*.

Do the market research to see what product or services your niche audience wants, then create for them something that will grab their attention. Now that we have potential product lines and services that your niche will love, lets jump into developing the movie you are going to create for them.

CHAPTER 9

Let's Make a Movie

All this talk about selling a movie and creating revenue streams is great but how do you make the film or product in the first place? Great question. Creating a film from scratch is beyond the scope of this book.

There are hundreds of books, online courses and workshops you can take to teach you the basics of film production. With that said, I thought I'd answer some burning questions I get asked all the time and also give you a few filmmaking hacks and case studies to get your feature film off the ground.

CASTING

Star power, do you need it to make a hit film? No. Can having a recognizable face help sell your film? Absolutely. Filmmakers sometimes put too much emphasis on cast. A great and marketable cast cannot guarantee box office success or that your film will be good. My short *BROKEN* had no recognizable faces in it but I was able to generate over $100,000 from an $8000 budget short film.

As the production costs go up you will need to hedge your bets and justify the more expensive budget and the hiring of marketable actors. Many film producers lean too heavily on hiring name actors and don't do the research on other elements that will help them take their projects to the marketplace.

Hiring name talent is surprisingly more affordable than you might think. Many actors who have market value overseas can be hired for one or two shooting days. The costs vary but you can hire these actors from between $2000 a day to $15,000 for a week. This is on a case by case basis but it never hurts to ask.

If your director has a good track record, that helps. If your shoot is in the town where they live and the actor doesn't have to fly out somewhere, that also helps. If your film is in an exotic location like Hawaii or Miami and they've always wanted to go there, that also helps. If you are trying to hire a name actor to come to Buffalo, NY in the winter for a $2000 day gig, I wish you the best of luck.

GENRE

Picking your genre is as important, if not more important, than your cast. The genre will determine your niche audience as well as if there's a market for ancillary products or services, and if the cast will be a major part of the film's equation.

If you pick a genre like horror, then the cast will have little or no impact on the marketability of the film, but I'll say it again - its always a plus to have an actor in your film who people recognize. Horror is one of the most affordable genres to make a film in. Think *Evil Dead*, *Paranormal Activity* or *The Blair Witch Project*. With that affordability also comes immense competition so keep that in mind.

If you choose the action genre, then you will need to spend money on cast or action. If you have ever walked the halls of the *American Film Market* you've probably seen what I'm talking about. We'll go over film markets in chapter 16.

Low budget action films with one key actor who people recognize, will help with international sales. If you have no name actors then you will need a ton of action spectacles. Some genres need marketable actors and others do not. Pick wisely my friend, this one decision can make or break your investment.

OUTSIDE THE BOX CASTING

The hit independent film *Range 15* is a horror comedy about soldiers fighting off a zombie apocalypse. Horror comedies are a tough sell in the marketplace but *Range 15* was able to make over $3,000,000 in gross revenue plus countless other streams of revenue selling ancillary products. Did I mention that this was the filmmaker's first film?

Since they were targeting a niche audience, which happened to be military veterans, they were able to cast real Army Rangers, Navy Seals and medal of honor winners who are extremely well-known in their community. They were basically the only film catering to that niche, a true blue ocean. More on Range 15 in chapter 11.

FEATURE FILM HACKING

One of the main keys to being a successful Filmtrepreneur is to keep your overhead or start-up costs low. This means keeping the budget of your film as low as possible, while still being able to create a viable product for the marketplace. So many first-time filmmakers make the mistake of going all in on their very first feature film.

Let's say I want to build a house from scratch. I watch those home improvement shows on TV so I think I can pull it off. Instead of trying to build a small shack in my backyard for a few bucks to see if I can actually build something that is beautiful and safe, I go big and decide to build a 4000-square-foot-home, with someone else's money. The chances of you constructing a house that is structurally safe and ready for the market is extremely slim.

Mark and Jay Duplass understood the concept of low overhead with their debut feature film *Puffy Chair*. The film was made for a $15,000 budget, which they borrowed from their parents. Every actor was paid $100 per day. They didn't shoot using a proper screenplay because at the budget level they were at would have been extremely difficult to do. The brothers opted to use a "scriptment" and had the actors improvise their lines.

What is a scriptment you ask? My definition of a scriptment is a very structured outline that has all the scenes of a film laid out with character motivations, scene goals, and has the overall arc of the entire film. The actors have the freedom to improvise the dialog as long as they hit the story beats of each scene.

In other words the actor has to get from point A to point B and how they get there is up to them and the director. Using this method really frees up the actors to have fun and play around with their character. If you want to see an example of a scriptment go to www.filmtrepreneur. com/bonus.

Puffy Chair went on to world premiere at the Sundance Film Festival and grossed over $195,000 at the theatrical box office. The film has gone on to generate revenue year after year and was even one of the first films licensed by a small start-up streaming service called Netflix.

The Duplass' didn't wait for a huge camera package, big name stars or even a screenplay. The budget was low enough that they could take the chance and shoot their feature film in that manner. By keeping the budget low they could move quickly, experiment and at the end of the day finish their film. They had a viable product for the marketplace they made it in record time.

Puffy Chair literally was the foundation that the brothers built their entire filmmaking empire on. They have gone on to produce studio films, HBO and Netflix features and series. For more on the Duplass Brothers' adventures in Hollywood read their stellar book *Like Brothers*.

This method is an extremely fast and efficient way of shooting a micro or low budget feature film. As the director and/or producer of your film you'll need to find actors who feel comfortable working this way. The scriptment method goes against the traditional ways actors are trained to perform in front of a camera.

If the actor is not ready or scared to put him or herself out there like this it will destroy your film so make sure to pick actors and crew members who are open-minded and willing to go on the journey with you.

On my first film *This is Meg* I used this technique and it worked extremely well. I was blessed to collaborate with some of the most seasoned and professional improv actors in Hollywood. My star and co-producer Jill-Michelle Meléan called her stand-up comic friends, asked if they wanted to come out for a day or so to have some fun and boom we had a cast. I shot the film in 8 days with a crew of three to four people.

Sometimes it was just myself, Jill and the camera. When we had more than one actor on set I would just work the story beats out with the actors and then went to light the scene. I was also the cinematographer, camera operator, gaffer and key grip among other jobs I did on the film.

I love this process so much that I shot my second film *On the Corner of Ego and Desire,* a film shot entirely at the Sundance Film Festival while the festival was going on, using the same scriptment/improv method. More on that film later in the book.

I had the pleasure of interviewing for my podcast filmmakers Ivan Malekin and Sarah Jayne. They shot their entire feature film *Friends, Foes and Fireworks* in one night (twenty four hours), filmed on the craziest and most chaotic nights of the year, New Years Eve. They relied entirely on improvisation and the use of a scriptment. They went on to sell the film internationally and even created an online course teaching their filmmaking techniques.

This method is just one filmmaking hack that can jump-start your project. Now, this process doesn't work on all film projects. It has to make sense for the story you are trying to tell. With that said, it came out in the press that Marvel's megabit film *Iron Man,* a $200 million budget feature film, had a lot of improvisation by the actors.

Here's what Oscar-Winning® actor Jeff Bridges said about his experience working on *Iron Man,* "It turned out that many times — 10, 12, 15 times — we would show up for the day's work, not knowing what we were gonna shoot. All the guys in the studio tapping their feet, looking at their watch, and we're sitting in my trailer trying to figure out my lines, man. – On the day!" You never know what will work until you try it.

I hope these ideas help you to get started on shooting your feature film project. I can teach you all about how to create revenue from a film but if you don't have a product to sell, then it makes it a bit more challenging to become a Filmtrepreneur.

– CASE STUDY –

This is Meg

I know it's hard to believe for many of you reading this but not only can you make a $5000 feature film but you can also make money with said film project. I made my first feature film *This is Meg* for about $5000 in 2017. Using the platform Seed and Spark, I crowdfunded about $9000 in cash and another $6000 in kind services, so when I started shooting my film I was already in the black.

We shot the film in eight days over the course of six weeks to work around the cast's schedule. Now, how did I pull this off, with a lot of help from my collaborators? How did I get there and why did it take so long for me to direct my first feature film?

Movie Poster for This is Meg

The story goes that in 2017 I was attached to another big film project with some heavy hitters in Hollywood. I was already casting for the film when the entire project fell apart, again. This was not the first time I was attached to a high profile feature film only to have it fall apart. If you read my first book *Shooting for the Mob* you'll see the most extreme version of a film project going through development hell and almost killing me in the process, literally.

When my most recent project took me for a ride again I had a serious talk with myself, "Alex you are not twenty-one anymore, you are almost forty years old. Tomorrow you'll wake up and be seventy years old, angry, and pissed off at the world. You can't keep doing this. It's time to make your first feature film. Stop making excuses. I know you are scared but if you don't do it you will become an angry and bitter filmmaker."

At that moment I decided I needed to make a film no matter what. Before my mind had a chance to talk me out of it, I called my dear friend Jill-Michelle Meléan, who happens to be a very talented stand-up comic and actress. I told her I was going to make a movie and wanted her to star in it.

It would be a story about her life as a kinda famous actress struggling to make it in Hollywood in the new world of social media likes, follows and influencers. I hadn't even finished my sentence when she said yes. I explained the way I wanted to make the film. No screenplay, using a scriptment, and backing into the story based on the locations, people, and resources we had. She was on board and we went to work.

Shooting a scene with Jill-Michele Meléan on the set of This is Meg

Thirty days later we were shooting the first scenes. Jilly called all of her amazingly talented friends and asked them to be in the film. They all said yes. Jilly's friends also happen to be some of the most talented improv actors and stand-up comics in the business with credits like Reno 911, Mad TV, Comedy Central and even Avatar. As they say, jump and the universe will send you a net.

We were off and running. It was an amazingly freeing experience. I didn't attach any outcome to the film's success. For me this was an experiment to see if I could direct a feature film. At such a low cost and having all of my budget crowdfunded I was free to have fun and take time to see what would work.

After 20 years directing commercials, music videos, award winning short films and editing/delivering over 60 feature films I still didn't believe I could do it. Your mind is your best friend and worst enemy all at the same time.

The shoot went off without a hitch. I shot the film with a 3-4 person crew. Everyone wore multiple hats. I had an old Blackmagic Cinema Camera 2.5K, some basic microphones, a sound recorder, some LED lights, and a basic set of camera lenses. I did a bunch of camera tests and felt I could capture a beautiful image with the gear I already owned.

On the set of This is Meg

My friend let me borrow a second Blackmagic Cinema Camera 2.5K for the shoot so now we could shoot twice as much coverage in less time. I also decided to be the cinematographer on the film as well, something I had never done before. I kinda wanted to overload my brain so it wouldn't have time to talk me out of moving forward as it had so many times in the past.

We generally never shot longer than six hours in a day and on our busiest day we shot a standard 10-12-hour day. The cast and crew had a great time. The scriptment method was a dream. The actors had a ball, I was a kid in a candy store and the footage was looking amazing. I finished editing, sound design and color grading the film within a couple of months.

I need to state something here. I was able to pull off making a feature film at this budget because I did a lot of the heavy lifting behind the camera. I was not only the director and cinematographer but I was also the camera man, sound man, assistant camera, editor, colorist, online editor, post-production supervisor, trailer editor, website designer, marketing specialist, and film festival adviser. I was able to do all of this because I had picked up those skills over twenty years in the business. I was putting new tools in my toolbox all the time.

Can you produce a feature film at this budget without these tools in your toolbox? Yes. Will it be more challenging? Yes. You'll need to partner up with people who have these skill sets. Jill had depth in casting, her story, some locations, and helped me produce *This is Meg*. I couldn't have made this film without her and vice versa.

Always try to pay everyone something for the day's work. Maybe if they help you as a crew member on your film you will return the favor on their film. Make a deal, be creative. If you can't pay the crew offer them a percentage of the total net revenue from the sales of the film. There's always a way.

Looking at Dailies with Joseph Reitman and Jill-Michele Meléan on the set of This is Meg

This is Meg went on to world premiere at the Cinequest Film Festival. After a short film festival run I decided to self-distribute the film. I did get offers from traditional distributors but I wanted to go through the process of self-distribution.

Through a film aggregator I put the film on all the major TVOD platforms as well as licensing the SVOD rights to Hulu.com. After the initial release I partnered with a traditional distributor for international sales. I didn't have a way to distribute internationally so I felt that partnership made sense. We sold the film to multiple territories and generated additional sales.

Now, thinking as a Filmtrepreneur, I also created multiple revenue streams for the film as well. I opened The IFH Masters Circle, a membership site where I took my members behind the scenes of how I made the film in addition to other original content. I then launched *Indie Film Hustle TV* (www.indiefilmhustle.tv), a streaming service that is Netflix for filmmakers, screenwriters and content creators.

I sell and rent *This is Meg* through the *IFHTV* platform and stream it as part of the membership. The making and distribution stories of *This is Meg* became a staple on the *Indie Film Hustle Podcast* helping me create multiple pieces of content through the podcast and my main blog IndieFilmHustle.com, which I was able to monetize.

Finally, I am writing about the making of the film in this book which is helping me create another revenue stream. I plan to release more course materials, workshops, and online education based on the making and distribution of *This is Meg*.

I want you to believe that in today's world there's always a way to produce your streaming series, video content or feature film. It's all about your own beliefs and mindset. The story I told myself for twenty years was that I was not ready to make my feature film yet. Bottom line I was scared. It stopped me from making my dream come true.

I'm certainly not the only filmmaker to make a micro-budget feature film that becomes successful. If we can do it so can you, and with the techniques I'm illustrating in this book you can create and monetize your own feature films and become a true Filmtrepreneur.

CHAPTER 10

Finding That Money

One of the biggest misconceptions in the indie film world is that finding money for your film is hard; it is and it isn't. Depending on your point of view financing your film might be the toughest or easiest part of the process. Film financing expert, Franco Sama says it best "Getting the money isn't the hard part…getting the money back is the hard part."

If you create projects that you can finance by yourself then finding money is not hard at all. If you create a project that needs $10 million and you have no experience producing films and want to direct, then finding money will be near impossible.

As a Filmtrepreneur it is in your best interest to keep your overhead as low as possible. The lower the budget, the faster you can be in profit. As I stated earlier it is a balancing act: keep the budget low but make sure you have enough to create a viable product for the marketplace.

The filmmaker's ego is never more delusional than when it is looking for money. The dream overtakes him and that dreaded "lottery ticket" mentality kicks in. They pray to meet that one person who can recognize their genius and finance their dreams. I don't mean to be harsh but I've just seen this scenario play out too many times.

I, too, have hunted for money to finance my filmmaking dreams over the years. I wasted so much time trying to raise money in the wrong way. Many of the mistakes I will lay out for you I made myself or saw others make. I was chasing money for one of my projects for over five years. Came close many times but it just never materialized.

It was all that frustration that convinced me that I needed to stop chasing money and start making movies. I began to tailor my stories for the budgets and resources I could finance myself. I started small then grew, experimented and had fun because the money was mine to lose. I had full creative control and I never looked back. Producing my small indie films was not only great for me but financially profitable as well.

The road I took was one of many options available to filmmakers today. Let's discuss mistakes to avoid when chasing that money.

A SCREENPLAY IS NOT ENOUGH

A big mistake I see again and again when filmmakers are in the raising money stage is to go out in search of money when they only have a script and a dream. They believe that the screenplay is so good that an investor is going to hear the pitch and just write them a check.

This is not how the business works. The screenplay is, of course, one of the foundations but having a great screenplay is not enough. I've personally read screenplays from accomplished screenwriters who can't get financing. I don't tell you this to discourage you, I tell you this so you have a realistic view of the marketplace.

ALL I NEED IS $10 MILLION

Many filmmakers will create a film with a budget of $5 million, $10 million or even $20 million. There are a few problems with attempting to raise this size budget. Many times these projects have a novice director with no track record attached or actors with no market value. You will be wasting your time and money if you go down this path.

Another issue is that the independent film marketplace has changed so much since the massive decline of the DVD market. Before that, you could produce a larger budget film and recoup the investment from DVD sales. The independent films that are getting financed are in the range of $150,000 to $3 million.

The higher the budget goes the more marketable the cast needs to be so the film can be sold overseas. To get an independent film financed over $3 million is extremely rare unless you have major stars attached and an experienced director and production team. Even then the budget of those films wouldn't go into the tens of millions.

The studios aren't making $10, $20 or even $50 million projects as much as they used to. Sure, there is the occasional Blumhouse horror film or outlier success story but professional screenwriter, Diane Drake, said it best, "The studios are in the business of making $300 million films that make $1 billion dollars back not making a $50 million film to make $150 million in return, generally speaking."

LETTERS OF INTENT

If I had a dollar for every time a filmmaker told me they had an LOI or letter of intent from a big star I'd be able to finance the next Marvel film myself. I don't know where this started but I want to debunk the notion that having an LOI is all you need to get your film financed.

A letter of intent is basically a one page document that states the actor in question is possibly interested in working on your project if their quote is met and scheduling permits.

In other words, it means absolutely nothing. An LOI can be put together by an actor's agent, manager or attorney. Many times the actor hasn't even read the script. If the money shows up then the actor might take it seriously but it is not legally binding. If you present an LOI to a film financier, more than likely they will run the other way. Savvy film investors understand how worthless it is.

THE PRE-SALE MYTH

In the olden days you could finance a film purely on international pre-sales. Pre-sales is when you go to a film market, pitch your idea with the cast you have in mind, show a movie poster you mocked up to a buyer and pre-sell that territory. So if you pre-sell the film rights to Germany, lets say, and you receive, $45,000 up front for that territory, you can use that money to help finance the film.

Once you do that a few times you would have the budget in place and then you can make offers to the actors you had in mind and you would be off and running. This technique was good for raising part of the budget or the entire thing.

Many filmmakers still think this practice is going on but, alas, not as often as they might believe. Because of streaming and the collapse of the DVD home video market there isn't as much money to go around. Add to that the scores of indie films being dumped on the marketplace monthly and you can see why buyers aren't willing to take a chance on pre-sales as much anymore.

Do indie films still get financed with pre-sales? Yes. Does it happen often? No. If a film producer is able to pre-sell a territory for an unproduced film it's because there is a relationship there built over years and more often than not the film buyer and producer have done many deals before.

Now that we have gone over what not to do let's discuss tips to raise money for your indie film.

HAVE SKIN IN THE GAME

Nobody likes to be the first one to the party and that is never more true than when you are looking to raise money for your film. If you want to speed up the process you should try to put in 20%-30% of the budget yourself. Many people have access to money around them and they don't even try. You, your family and friends might be able to chip in and if they can't they might know someone who can.

You would be surprised what happens when you just ask. If you pitch an investor and you walk in with skin in the game it automatically proves to them that you believe in this project. Also, if you add money to the film you have more say on what happens. This will set you apart from every other filmmaker trying to raise the entire budget on his own from outside investors.

TAX CREDITS

In the 90's, states in the US, started to grant tax credit incentives to entice film producers to shoot their projects in their states. If a production moved to the state the producers would save money on taxes owed. The tax credit would range from 15% up to 45% or higher in some international countries. This would bring jobs and millions of dollars into that state's local economy.

In the beginning state film commissions would be more than happy to speak to any independent film producer who brought them a project. They would spend tons of man-hours helping the producer with paperwork and getting everything ready for the production to start.

The problem was that many productions just never materialized and all that time and money would have been wasted by the film commission. Nowadays, film commissions won't even speak to you unless you have "proof of funds." You need to prove to the film commission that you have money in the bank to actually produce the film you want a tax credit for.

The state of Georgia allows for a 20% tax credit for production companies that spend $500,000 or more on film production or post-production in the state. This is why so many Hollywood films and series are shot in Georgia. If you play it correctly tax credits are a powerful way to help a feature film get financed.

CROWDFUNDING

The world changed the day crowdfunding was invented. Crowdfunding is the practice of funding a project, via a crowdfunding platform online, by small amounts of money from a large group of people.

You could now go straight to the audience you were trying to target and raise funds to develop that next great tech gadget, build a space age toaster or, of course, make a feature film.

With crowdfunding you can not only raise money but you get the bonus of building an audience that is vested in your success. If someone donates to your crowdfunding campaign there's a good chance they might be interested in not only your films but your ancillary products and services as well.

You can use platforms like Kickstarter and Indiegogo to launch your campaign but I recommend Seed and Spark. They are the only crowdfunding platform that is solely dedicated to helping filmmakers. I ran my first campaign for *This is Meg* using their platform and I couldn't have been happier with the results. For more tips on how to run a successful crowdfunding campaign go to www.filmtrepreneur.com/bonus.

SPONSORSHIPS AND PRODUCT PLACEMENT

Sponsorships and product placements are very overlooked ways of raising some capital for your film project. At a minimum, it's a way to get product you could use in the film.

If I'm finally going to produce my vegan chef film, *Crazy, Sexy, Vegan*, it would probably be a good idea to reach out to Beyond Meat, the leading provider of plant-based meat in America. If I have done my job as a Filmtrepreneur and cultivated a large audience of vegans, plant-based enthusiasts, and vegetarians, then this technique will work like a charm.

I can propose a partnership with Beyond Meat that would include some sponsorship money, product to use in my film, and soon to be released online cooking courses. In exchange, I would feature their product throughout the film, use their products in cooking courses, the film's website, social media accounts, trailers and posters.

Beyond Meat could further tap into my audience by giving them exclusive discounts on their products. I could also ask Beyond Meat to send out promotional emails to their massive list when the film is about to be released.

This partnership is a win-win for both Beyond Meat and me. They receive a ton of press and exposure while I add some money to my bottom line and get the added bonus of attaching a trusted brand in the targeted niche to my project. Even if money never exchanges hands, the product, the association, and the marketing push from the company would be amazing to have.

Think of what companies do business within your niche and see what kind of deal you can cut that benefits both of you.

CHAPTER 11

Buildng an Audience

The biggest mistake I see filmmakers make when attempting to build an audience is that they are broadcasting, yelling things, and asking for something all the time. When you meet someone at a party you just don't go up to them and say "Can you give me money for my film, here's my crowdfunding campaign, SUPPORT ME!"

Sounds crazy right? But that is exactly what most filmmakers do. They Instant Message people and ask for money, or can you read my script or watch my short film? You will not build an audience acting this way.

You need to understand that you have to provide value to your audience. You need to be of service and approach all your social media posts and interactions with this in mind.

There are three ways you can serve an audience.

1. You can educate
2. You can inspire
3. You can entertain

I have built my audience by leading with education, then following up with inspiration and finally entertaining them once in a while. That's the brand I have been building with Indie Film Hustle. You don't need to use all three, you can pick one method and double down on that.

You are creating a contract with your follower or subscriber which states, "If you follow me I will provide the service you are looking for. Whether entertaining, educational or inspirational content."

So many times I see filmmakers or brands that have no idea who or what they are. They're pumping out so many types of content that people just tune out because the brand has already broken that contract with the audience.

I started with educating my audience using podcast episodes, blog posts, and video content. As my audience grew I realized that many of my tribe was wanting me to create more inspirational content in addition to the educational so I did. Finally, I let my personality loose and I started posting funny quotes and videos that were designed specifically for my audience.

EDUCATION

People are always looking for ways to better themselves and with the flood of information available online it can get overwhelming. By positioning yourself or your brand as a resource for the type of content your audience is looking for, you will stand out from the crowd.

If you choose education as your means to cultivate your audience, you can create podcasts, videos, or written content. As you create this content you further establish yourself as an authority in your niche and with time you become a thought leader. You can use all forms of educational content or focus on one. YouTube creators use videos, bloggers use articles and podcasters use audio. Choose the one method that works best for the type of audience you are trying to cultivate.

INSPIRATIONAL

This is a very powerful way to cultivate an audience online. It seems like social media was designed specifically for inspirational content. There are social media accounts that have tens of millions of followers and all they do is pump out inspirational quotes, videos or other content. You can use quote cards to spread your inspirational message, which can be easily generated with Apps like Typeorama.

ENTERTAIN THEM

If you want to be front and center you can create a following by entertaining your audience with silly videos, singing, creating shows, etc. This method is more suited for the brand or person who wants to become a personality or influencer but you still need to provide value. Kim Kardashian has built a media empire using this method.

Her content is entertaining escapism. Her audience tunes into her content because it's escapist and voyeuristic. She has over 110 million followers on Instagram, over 60 million on Twitter and receives $500,000 per social media post. Love her or hate her, Mrs. Kardashian's audience wants to follow her and her family's escapades. She has taken entertainment content to a social media audience to the highest levels.

THE CURATOR

You don't always need to create content from scratch, you can become a "curator" of content. This means that you can do the legwork and scour the Internet for content that your audience would like to consume. There's a tremendous value in that.

If I'm a follower of yours and you provide me with excellent articles, videos, or podcasts that are interesting to me everyday, I will follow you.

THE PIGGYBACK METHOD

You can also piggyback on content that is extremely popular in the niche audience you are trying to cultivate. Let's say you are trying to establish yourself as a zombie horror brand or personality within that niche. Would it make sense for you to launch a *Walking Dead* podcast or YouTube show discussing each episode and targeting that niche audience with that content?

The Walking Dead is an extremely popular TV show in the zombie horror space and if you piggyback on its success you can jump-start your following. People who love *The Walking Dead* are rabid fans and want to consume as much content about the show as possible. If you are a filmmaker trying to produce a zombie indie film, could you tap that audience?

If they know and trust you because of the amazing zombie content you have been providing, it's safe to say they would probably be open to helping you spread the word about a zombie film that you are producing. They may even donate to your crowdfunding campaign and eventually purchase zombie themed films or products you create.

WHO IS YOUR AVATAR?

When I say avatar I'm not speaking of James Cameron's blockbuster film franchise, I'm referring to the avatar of your perfect customer. When you are starting your audience-building journey you need to clarify, to yourself, what kind of audience you are trying to cultivate.

I will use my vegan chef movie, *Crazy, Sexy, Vegan* as an example. If I know I want to create a film with ancillary products or services that will be targeting this niche I would begin to create my perfect avatar. I would give my avatar a name and build a profile for him or her by asking myself the following questions.

1. How old is my perfect avatar?
2. What kind of content does my avatar consume?
3. Where does my avatar hang out online?
4. What events or conventions does my avatar pay to attend?
5. What kind of job does my avatar have?
6. What is the yearly income of my avatar?
7. What are the dreams of my avatar?
8. What are my avatar's pain points I can help with?
9. What kind of products or services does my avatar purchase?

By creating your perfect avatar you will be better prepared to be of service to him or her. This avatar is just a sample of your audience. Not everyone in your audience will check off all these boxes but you will better understand who you are targeting and can better create content that best suits the audience you are trying to attract and cultivate.

BLOGGING

Blogging is dead, not so fast. Creating a blog is still one of the most important things you can do when building an audience. Your blog is your hub for all things you. If you are posting articles on Facebook your audience has nowhere to go other than Facebook. By creating a blog or hub for all your content, then your audience has somewhere to go to discover more of your writing, video or audio content.

As you create more avenues of content, whether podcasts, videos on YouTube, writing, or images, all paths should lead back to your blog. I have members of my audience who discover an episode of my podcast or a video on YouTube and then visit my blog for the first time. There they discover a treasure trove of content that they more than likely would be interested in consuming. It's an extremely powerful way to make the connection with your audience even stronger.

EMAIL, EMAIL, EMAIL

Email, by far, is the most powerful way to connect with your audience. Generating an email list is imperative for a Filmtrepreneur. Creating an audience on Facebook, YouTube or any other platform is great but you do not have direct access to your audience.

If Facebook decides to stop showing your posts to your followers what would you do? By the way, this isn't hypothetical; this actually happened a few years ago. Facebook decided that they were going to change their website to a kind of pay-to-play platform meaning if you want to reach all of your followers you would have to pay for Facebook ads or boosts. This change destroyed business models overnight.

If you play in someone else's sandbox you will need to play by their rules. By having an email list you have a direct connection to your audience and potential customer. No middleman. No corporation controlling your access.

Use the social media platforms for what they are good for, which is looking for people interested in what you have to offer. The goal should be to drive those people to your blog or hub and capture an email address.

The basic system to capture emails is to create a lead generator. I used a free Film Distribution Survival Guide eBook on Filmtrepreneur. com. This is information that is extremely helpful and sought after by the audience I'm trying to target.

My Lead Generator on the Filmtrepreneur Website

If you are creating a horror brand you could create the Top 10 list of horror films you never heard of. If you create a website for the *Crazy, Sexy, Vegan*, you can create an eBook with top 10 easy plant-based recipes. You get the idea. Just create something that is irresistible to your target audience.

You will need an email marketing service to host your email list. A good email marketing service should have an easy to use interface, ideally drag & drop, and allow you to create highly engaging newsletters. There are many affordable options. Here are a few services you can use.

- GetResponse
- Mailchimp
- Constant Contact
- Convertkit
- AWeber
- Drip

Some are more expensive than others so pick the one that works the best for your needs.

PODCASTING

Launching a podcast is an amazing way to cultivate an audience. I've been able to build my tribe using the power of podcasting. To date I have three full-time podcasts in my niche of filmmaking and screenwriting, the *Indie Film Hustle Podcast*, the *Bulletproof Screenwriting Podcast* and the *Filmtrepreneur Podcast*. These podcasts have become so successful I plan to launch more in the future.

Podcasting is unique in the way it connects with an audience. Maintaining someone's attention for long periods of time is difficult for video creators but podcast listeners are used to listening for hours at a time, building a more intimate connection. Whether they are at the gym, driving, commuting to work or just walking, your voice is there with them. Podcasting should definitely be a tool in your audience building toolbox.

VIDEO CONTENT

Video content is one of the most popular types of content on the Internet. When you are scrolling down your social media feed what kind of content do you normally stop on? I'd bet to say it is a video. I know many filmmakers prefer to be behind the camera rather than in front of it. I completely understand. It took me a long time before I felt comfortable in front of the lens. That's probably why I started with podcasting as my content medium of choice.

If you really don't want to get in front of that camera you can create inspirational videos using stock footage, graphic only videos, or video essays. There are many options for creating compelling video content without being the star of the show. Find what works for you and start creating valuable content.

YOUTUBE

YouTube is the king of video content online. Not only is it the most used platform for video but it is also the second most used search engine in the world, behind Google of course. Another bonus to uploading your videos to YouTube is that Google prioritizes YouTube videos in its results. I get a tremendous amount of traffic from people clicking on my video via Google search results.

FACEBOOK VIDEO

Facebook Video is another amazing platform to upload your videos as well. If you post a YouTube video link on Facebook the algorithm doesn't give your post much love. But if you upload that same content to Facebook Video, the algorithm will get that video in front of more eyeballs.

IGTV

Instagram has jumped into the video content game. Known for being the photo content platform, Instagram decided to add video content as well. They launched IGTV where you can upload videos to different channels on your profile. Instagram is growing extremely fast and if you are targeting a younger demographic this is the place to be.

MICRO-CONTENT

I know what many of you are thinking, "Alex, this sounds great but how can I create so much content?" Well here's a tip, use micro-content. Let's say you have an hour interview you did with a thought leader in your space. The following are techniques to create 50-60 pieces of valuable content for your audience from just one interview that can be posted to your Facebook, Instagram, Twitter, YouTube, LinkedIn, Podcast and Blog.

- You can release the entire interview on YouTube.
- You can cut the video interview into smaller bite-sized clips and post them on your social media platforms.
- Take that interview and release the audio on your podcast.
- Create a blog post about your podcast interview.
- You can create audio clips with a graphic to post of social media.
- You can create quotes or inspirational cards, based on the interview, to post on all your social media platforms.
- You can have the interview transcribed to post on your blog and/or Medium.com.
- From that same transcription you can pull quotes that you can post directly onto your social media platforms.

As you can see, there are many ways to create compelling content to build an audience. Create value that is perfectly aligned with your audience's needs, solve your audience's problems, and always lead with being of service and you will be successful.

CROWDSOURCING

Crowdsourcing is a fairly new term in the marketing space. According to author, Richard Botto's remarkable book on the subject *Crowdsourcing for Filmmakers: Indie Film and the Power of the Crowd*, the term was originally defined in a June 2006 Wired magazine article, "The Rise of Crowdsourcing" by Jeff Howe.

He stated, "Simply defined, crowdsourcing represents the act of a company or institution taking the action once performed by employees and outsourcing it to an undefined (and generally large) network of people in the form of an open call." In other words you are outsourcing work to the crowd.

For a Filmtrepreneur, crowdsourcing is using the power of a niche audience to help you market, sell and eventually purchase a film, product or service you are selling. Understanding the power of the crowd, or niche audiences, can be extremely powerful as you are about to see.

Filmmaker, military veteran, businessman and YouTuber, Nick Palmisciano, understands this better than most. Nick is the co-founder of *Ranger Up*, an apparel company that designs and manufactures shirts for veterans and the people who love the men and women of the Armed Forces.

After becoming a leader in his niche space he created the Ranger Up YouTube channel that catered specifically to his niche audience of military, law enforcement, paramedics, fire fighters and veterans. The content he and his team created for the channel is extremely niche with inside jokes only his audience would understand. The channel's videos have been downloaded millions of times.

Making all these videos inspired the Ranger Up team to work on a feature film that their audience would enjoy. Nick and his fellow veterans were tired of how Hollywood portrayed soldiers in films, as well as the gross inaccuracies in uniforms and use of weapons.

Nick teamed up with Matt Best, the owner of a military-themed apparel company *Article 15 Clothing*. Together, they came up with *Ranger 15*, an apocalyptic zombie action comedy that the audiences they had built up over the years would love. To keep the film extremely authentic to their niche audience the filmmakers decided to cast real military veterans, medal of honor winners, and members of both companies in the film.

Ranger Up and *Article 15 Clothing* launched a crowdsourcing campaign on the crowdfunding platform *Indiegogo*, with a goal to raise

$325,000. The two companies mobilized their social media followings as well as creating amazing perk packages like an executive producer credit, digital downloads, t-shirts, being an extra in the film, and even being the film's ultimate hero.

The strategy worked. Within the first 24 hours they raised $120,000 and by the end of the week they had already reached their goal of raising $325,000. By the end of the campaign they were able to raise $1,140,300 from 10,797 backers to become the 4th largest campaign in the history of Indiegogo. With a larger budget they were able to cast some known actors like Danny Trejo, Sean Astin, Keith David and even *the* legendary William Shatner.

After the film was finished Nick and his partners met with many traditional distribution companies. Being businessmen the deals these companies were offering didn't make any business sense. They decided to self-distribute the film themselves using a film aggregator. They were able to get their film on the TVOD platforms iTunes and Amazon.

Once again they mobilized their audience and, on launch day, Ranger 15 rose to the top of the charts landing at #2 for all of iTunes. Ranking higher than all the big budget studio films recently released. Ranger 15 ended up generating over $3 million in sales, not to mention the revenue generated by ancillary products like t-shirts, hats and other merchandise. The film is still generating revenue to this day. After they had exhausted the self-distribution route they partnered with a traditional distributor that could release the film outside their core audience internationally.

This is a perfect example of crowdsourcing a niche audience. Now let's jump into making your film.

CHAPTER 12

Micro-Budget Filmmaking

As you know, another key concept of the Filmtrepreneur Method is to keep your overhead as low as possible, while still being able to create a marketable product. I've seen so many filmmakers spend ungodly amounts of money on an independent film with no understanding of how they are going to recoup their investment.

Let's look at producing a film as if we were going to produce a bottle of wine. When you create the product, you are trying to source the raw materials as cheaply as possible while maintaining quality. You would price out the cost of the bottle, labels, corks and the wine itself. You need to approach filmmaking in the same manner. I understand that one is a product and films are an art form but the principles are the same.

As the producer, you need to hire talent and crew that give you the biggest bang for the buck. For example, hiring a cinematographer who owns or has access to a camera and lighting kit and who can package a deal for everything is a good bang for your buck. Just make sure he or she can produce the quality of work you need to create a sellable film.

TOOLS IN THE TOOLBOX

When I set out to direct my first feature film I didn't want to pursue that golden carrot I'd been chasing for most of my filmmaking career. I didn't want to package another feature film, try to attach talent, make a proof of concept short for it, and of course hunt for money to be able to make the film. I'd wasted decades playing that game.

If I may quote the masterpiece baseball film *Bull Durham*, "It's a simple game. You throw the ball, catch the ball, hit the ball." Keeping that in mind I asked myself what was the bare minimum I needed to create a feature film. A camera, lenses, sound equipment, lights, locations, actors, and a story to tell.

While other people were playing the game by rules set down by the establishment I was writing my own rules shooting *This is Meg*. Film-making is an extremely difficult path to walk. People will tell you that you need this camera and that amount of crew to make a "real" film. You need to be a rebel, to think differently, this is one of the most important advantages you have on your path.

Indie film legend Robert Rodriguez, who signed a deal at the age of twenty-three for his $7000 feature film *El Mariachi*, played by his own rules even after he was invited into the studio system. He set up his production offices in Austin, TX away from Hollywood to maintain his freedom.

Even when offered film budgets millions more than he knew he needed he always approached each project with the mentality of an indie filmmaker. He kept his budgets as low as he could while making a marketable product for the marketplace. This is why his career has endured while many of his contemporaries had very short-lived journeys.

The Filmtrepreneur thinks of his or her audience first and then creates a product that his or her audience will love to consume. We all need to start somewhere. Don't think you need to compete with a $200 million studio blockbuster when you are trying to make your first film. Start small, learn from your mistakes and most importantly, get up and make something, don't just talk about it.

– CASE STUDY –

For Lovers Only

What if I told you that a pair of filmmakers produced an indie film on no budget, shot with a 1st generation DSLR camera in black and white and self-distributed the film, which went on to generate over $500,000 in revenue. Hard to believe, right? That's exactly what filmmakers Michael and Mark Polish did with their film *For Lovers Only*.

The Polish Brothers have been making independent films, on their own terms, for over a decade now. Since premiering at the Sundance Film Festival with their debut feature, 1999's *Twin Falls Idaho*, the brothers have remained steadfast in their commitment to creating personal, character-driven films.

Michael Polish has created a filmography of critically-acclaimed features, including the karaoke-themed *Jackpot* (2001), the self-financed period piece *Northfork* (2003) and the sci-fi drama *The Astronaut Farmer* (2006). Yet the Polish brothers have always maintained a collaborative— as opposed to competitive—spirit when it comes to finding success in Hollywood. In 2005, the brothers published the must-read book *The Declaration of Independent Filmmaking: An Insider's Guide to Making Movies Outside of Hollywood*, a how-to guide for first-time filmmakers.

The film came from a screenplay that Mark Polish wrote more than a decade ago called *For Lovers Only*, about an American photographer who runs into an old flame while on assignment in Paris. The film follows the rekindled lovers around Paris, France in a series of quiet vignettes that slowly reveal more about each of the couple's complicated lives.

Inspired by the guerrilla style of the French New Wave filmmakers of yesteryear, Mark and Michael Polish came up with a simple plan: they'd fly over to France with only a Canon 5D Mark II camera, which they already owned, and one actress, Stana Katic, who is known from the hit television show *Castle*, in tow and just go out and shoot a feature film.

With no budget to speak of, they went out into Paris and captured its stunning beauty for free. Additionally, shooting solely on a DSLR had quite a few advantages. Not only was the camera extremely portable, and allowed for filming in tight spaces, such as the small alcoves in French churches, it also gave the film the level of intimacy it needed. No one stopped them since they were such a small crew and the camera was a still camera, with video capabilities, everyone thought they were a married couple simply on vacation.

Screenwriter and actor Mark Polish explained the process. "It was me, Mike and Stana, and that was it. We shot for 12 days, and the whole point was to capture this really intense intimacy between the two characters."

The brothers said that their hotels and some meals were comped; they shot and edited with the equipment they already owned; and they don't consider the few grand worth's of meals, taxis and the like to be part of an actual budget. "There was not one dime that came out of our pocket specifically for this movie — besides the food we ate, but we had to eat, anyway," stated Mark Polish.

This proves that you don't need a ton of money and equipment to make an indie feature film. I know what you are thinking, "but they were established filmmakers with major credits and had a popular TV actress as the lead." Yes, but the way they shot and distributed the film was straight indie without question. In chapter 19 I'll discuss the marketing and self-distribution plan that generated the brothers over $500,000 in revenue.

CRASHING SUNDANCE

After my success with *This is Meg* I wanted to challenge myself even more than I did before. *This is Meg* was produced for around $5000, shot in very controlled environments, using extremely experienced actors, over the course of an eight day shoot. As you can tell by now I like a challenge so I decided my next project would be a bit more adventurous. That challenge came in my next film *On the Corner of Ego and Desire*.

This film would test me in ways I had never been tested before. Why not shoot a narrative feature film for a budget of around $3000, at the Sundance Film Festival, which had never been done before, while the festival was going on, cast young and talented actors over Skype, using a scriptment, with a crew of four people, over the course of four days in freezing cold temperatures.

Because the budget was so low I had the freedom to experiment and have fun. I felt no pressure and knew I could pull off something of value for my niche audience of filmmakers and screenwriters.

Shooting a scene in the middle of a real party for
On the Corner of Ego and Desire

On the Corner of Ego and Desire is about three hapless independent filmmakers who make the trek to the Sundance Film Festival and go through absolute hell in searching for an elusive producer who is supposedly going to buy their independent feature film, all within 24 hours. Ignorance, foolishness and above all ego, drive the team to implosion as they struggle to realize their filmmaking dreams. I couldn't have designed a film more perfectly for my audience.

My producing partner Adam Bowman and I flew to Sundance with my trusty four-man crew, which included my cinematographer Austin Nordell, the location sound engineer Kile Stumbo and all-around go to helper Straw Weisman, and me.

We met the actors there and the adventure began. The cast, crew and I first sat down and worked out the scriptment so we would have a solid foundation to jump off from. I had been to Sundance many times before so I knew the lay of the land. As I was writing the film I knew where in Park City we could shoot scenes.

Looking for a battery on Main Street shooting
On the Corner of Ego and Desire

We shot the film with one camera, the Blackmagic Pocket Cinema Camera 1080p model on a mono-pod using a Sigma 18-35mm photo lens and a couple of vintage cinema lenses I purchased on eBay to give the movie a more 90's Super 16mm indie film look. 90% of the film was shot outside using available light but I brought one LED light that we would bounce off the walls for interior night shots.

I would give the actors 3-4 takes per set up and then we would move on. The entire film was shot in a guerrilla style with no permits and completely run and gun. My theory was that during the film festival there would be hundreds of camera crews running up and down Main Street so we could just blend in. I made sure to keep a small footprint so we wouldn't draw attention to ourselves and be able to move quickly.

DP Austin Nordell lines up a scene with Rob Alicea for
On the Corner of Ego and Desire

It wasn't all pirate filmmaking. If we would shoot a scene in a restaurant we would ask the owner for permission. What was a pleasant surprise was that every place we would shoot, people around us were so kind and accommodating. If we jumped on a bus the bus driver would turn off the music, if we wanted to go to the second floor of a restaurant to shoot outside, no problem. The film Gods were with us for sure.

Setting up a shot at ground zero of Sundance

The ultimate shot in the film is a wide angle of the iconic Egyptian movie theater on Main Street in Park City. Actress Sonja O'Hara, the cinematographer, and I, woke up around 4:00a.m. and we went down to Main Street to grab the shots. When we got there the entire street was empty, no cars were moving, all the lights were on and there was a light snow flurry falling. It couldn't be any more perfect. It was like having our own personal Sundance backlot.

I knew shooting at the Sundance Film Festival, while the festival was going on, would give the film an amazing amount of production value. Whenever you can shoot at a location or event that is live you benefit from its inherent production value. Shooting at a live carnival, parade, or convention are all great locations.

Shooting a scene for On the Corner of Ego and Desire

All in all we figured out that we shot for a total of 36 hours, I was still doing interviews for my podcast so I was filming on the side. I flew home and began the editing process. I finished editing, color grading and mastering the entire film in Davinci Resolve, an extremely powerful piece of post-production software that any Filmtrepreneur can download for free at www.filmtrepreneur.com/bonus.

On the Corner of Ego and Desire went on to world premiere at the Raindance Film Festival in the United Kingdom and even got a screening at the world famous Chinese Theater in Hollywood, CA. I partnered with a trusted traditional distributor to release the film on Amazon, Apple TV, Google and all the other major TVOD, SVOD and AVOD platforms. The film also lives on my streaming service *Indie Film Hustle TV* (www.indiefilmhustle.tv).

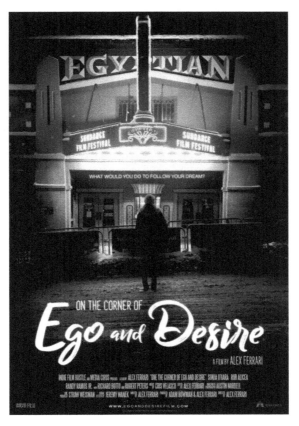

Movie poster of On the Corner of Ego and Desire.
Design by Dan Cregan and Alex Ferrari

Just by making this film I have already generated revenue by leveraging my online platforms IndieFilmHustle.com and Filmtrepreneur.com. I've released content like podcast episodes, articles and trailers. I plan to create online courses and live workshops teaching my methods for producing micro-budget feature films. I will be creating ancillary products like posters and t-shirts as well. And, of course, I've used the making of the film as content for this book.

I hope this case study inspires you to go out and make your own *On the Corner of Ego and Desire*. The technology has never been more affordable to produce a feature film. Don't be afraid of take risks, as long as that budget stays low. I built this film specifically for my niche audience and, because I know them so well, I knew I could take some risks as long as I brought them something that would entertain, educate, and inspire.

CHAPTER 13

The Money is in the Lunchboxes

As legendary filmmaker George Lucas once said "The money is in the lunchboxes." He, of course, is referring to the billions of dollars he sold in ancillary products from his *Star Wars* franchise. Lucas was one of the first Filmtrepreneurs. He was thinking outside the box before Hollywood had a chance to catch up.

His deal with 20th Century Fox was so legendary that it changed how film industry contracts are written to this day. In the agreement Lucas passed up on a $500,000 directing fee and in return he held onto the rights to make sequels to the *Star Wars* films but, more importantly, he kept the licensing and merchandising rights to all the characters and films. In other words, he can sell t-shirts, action figures and, of course, lunchboxes based on the movies.

To date, *Star Wars* merchandise has made over $45 billion and adds an estimate $1.5 billion each year. Not bad for a filmmaker in the right place at the right time.

We can learn something from George Lucas and his success with *Star Wars*. As Filmtrepreneurs we need to think about those ancillary products, those product lines that can be sold to a customer who is hungry for our wares. Here are a few ideas for product lines you can create with companies that can help you make and distribute them.

T-SHIRTS AND STUFF

You can create products like t-shirts, apparel, hats, and posters through companies like CafePress.com and TeeSpring.com. These companies allow you not to have any upfront costs so you can create an entire run of products easily and for free. They do take a bigger chunk off the back-end but you don't need to worry about buying inventory, setting up a distribution center to mail out products or dealing with customer service. They take care of it all.

This is a great way for Filmtrepreneurs to test the market and see what their customer base wants. If sales explode, then you might want to set up a more traditional merchandise company to grab more profit but you'll need to set up all the infrastructure that I laid out before.

STRATEGIC PARTNERSHIPS

Once you have identified your niche audience, investigate what companies and products are being sold in that space. You can reach out to those companies and offer a strategic partnership with your film. By doing this, you will add credibility to your project by partnering with a company that is well respected in the space.

Some of the ways to leverage this partnership for the benefit of both parties is as follows:

- Asking the company to help you promote the film through their social media channels and email list
- Possibly having the company purchase ads and airtime to promote their products in association with your film.
- Offer discounts to the products or services of the company to people who purchase or rent your film
- Have product placement of the product, service, or company's name in the film itself

There are many ways to structure a strategic partnership deal. In the end any deal must be beneficial to both parties. Joe Cross, the filmmaker behind the game-changing documentary *Fat, Sick and Nearly Dead* did just that with his strategic partner Breville Juicers.

Cross approached Breville and offered a partnership deal. He would put their juicer in his documentary and only promote their brand of juicer. When the film was released Breville juicer sales exploded. I, personally, was inspired by Joe's documentary and what brand of juicer did I buy? Breville because it was the juicer he was using in the documentary. It was brilliant product placement.

When I went to the store, *Bed, Bath and Beyond*, to purchase my juicer, what was sitting right next to the display but a DVD of *Fat, Sick and Nearly Dead*, which you got for free when you purchased the juicer. Brilliant!

– CASE STUDY –

Pool Party Massacre

Filmmaker Drew Marvick is the writer/director of an 80's style horror indie film called *Pool Party Massacre*. Drew's story is the perfect Filmtrepreneur example. *Pool Party Massacre* was created for the niche audience he knew the best because he is a card carrying member of the niche, 80's style horror film fans. When he set out to create his film he knew his audience better than most.

It took him over a year to complete his film, shooting on weekends, pulling favors from friends and trying to make it happen. Since it was shot over such a long period of time some of the actors' hair changed, the weather went from summer to winter and a ton of other continuity issues were scattered throughout the film.

The amazing thing is that all these "mistakes" worked perfectly for the kind of film Drew was trying to make. His niche audience loves to watch those kinds of mistakes because the films they grew up watching in the 80's had all of those issues.

This is why having a deep understanding of your chosen niche audience is so important. If you could create something for a niche that you, yourself, are a part of, all the better. Drew knew that it was going to be a challenge to get any sort of attention for his little horror film so he started to think like a Filmtrepreneur. First thing he did was to reach out to poster artist Marc Schoenbach to create retro poster art for his indie film.

Movie Poster for Pool Party Massacre.
Art by Marc Schoenbach

Schoenbach, owns Sadist Art Designs and is well respected by Drew's niche audience. Schoenbach creates retro '80s artwork that is reminiscent of those amazing 80's VHS covers. His artwork has adorned the covers of 80's classic horror films like *The Barn* and *The Diabolical.*

Drew realized this was going to be one of the keys to making his micro-budget horror film stand out. He commissioned a painting for the poster and cover art for the film. Marc Schoenbach's artwork for *Pool Party Massacre* channeled the spirit of that nostalgic 80's VHS cover art.

Never underestimate the power of good movie poster artwork. Now that Drew had artwork that would grab the attention of his niche audience he started to implement the Filmtrepreneur Method. He asked the question, what products does my niche audience love to purchase? He came up with an impressive list of ancillary products.

- Colored VHS Special Editions
- Metal Lunch Boxes
- T-Shirts, Hats, Aprons
- Beer Cozies
- Branded Drinking Glasses
- Physical media: Blu-Rays, DVDs
- Posters
- Enamel Pins
- Limited Edition Action Figures

Yes, an action figure. Drew commissioned a company that makes handcrafted action figures. They created a figure of the headless blue bikini character from the film. He sold each figure for $45 apiece and sold out. He also created other product lines that his niche would love.

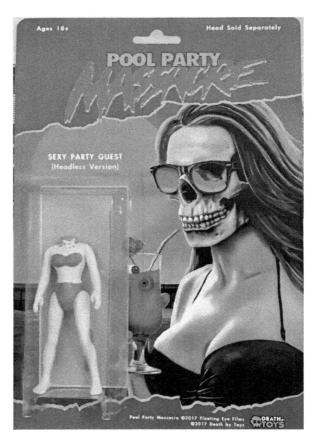

Headless blue bikini character toy from Pool Party Massacre

From the 80's staple metal lunch boxes, to movie posters to enamel pins to beer cozies. The artwork was so perfectly aligned with the niche audience that many customers purchased the posters and copies of the film thinking it was an actual 80's horror classic they happened to have missed.

Ancillary product lines for the film Pool Party Massacre

Drew even created ancillary products that weren't directly related to his film but were within the scope of his niche audience. Hats and enamel pins that said 'I LOVE 80'S HORROR' and 'I LOVE INDIE HORROR.'

Spill off products that cater to the niche audience

He was tapping into a spillover niche of customers who might not purchase merchandise from his film but might buy a product that represents what they love. Both audiences would be attracted by his amazing artwork and once he had their attention he tried to sell them another product line. This is Filmtrepreneur 101.

T-shirts and other products from Pool Party Massacre

My favorite product that Drew created is the limited edition colored VHS copies of the film. Talk about nostalgia. The first question I asked him was where he was getting those VHS tapes produced? His answered floored me. He would go around to thrift stores and garage sales in his area and buy out all the classic Disney animated films he could find on VHS. He would clean the VHS tapes of all the sticky goop and stickers, relabel them with *Pool Party Massacre* labels and then record over the Disney movie with his own film.

He had three limited edition runs of the film on VHS. Considering his access to colored VHS was limited he could only go so far with this without expanding and growing the business. He had great names for each of his production runs.

Staying on the brand of *Pool Party Massacre* he created the '*Algae Green*' edition, a green VHS, the '*Pee in the Pool*', a yellow VHS and the '*Super Rad Slip Box*' edition for the standard black VHS. These colors were based on what VHS inventory he found in his area.

Customer built vintage VHS copies of Pool Party Massacre

He was literally buying and selling nostalgia. By using a product line that his niche would recognize he leveraged their knowledge and love of the good old days. By doing this Drew also tapped into a very powerful marketing concept called association. Because his product was not only unique, but also nostalgic every time a new customer would see his product he would associate his film with the same quality level of other films wrapped in that packaging years ago.

When I saw his VHS cover and packaging for the first time I was transported back to my video store days where I was renting classic horror and thrillers on VHS. The association was remarkably powerful.

Now, this doesn't work for everything. Putting your film on DVD because you think you'll tap into some DVD nostalgia might not work because, as of the writing of this book, DVDs are still being used and it wouldn't have the same nostalgic power that say 70's era bell-bottom jeans would have.

THINK OUTSIDE THE PRODUCT BOX

When thinking of product lines for your film think outside of the box. Sure, t-shirts, hats, pins, stickers, and posters are the low-hanging fruit but just like Drew Marvick did with *Pool Party Massacre*, create unique products that your audience will love. The limited edition VHS versions of his film, was a genius move.

Headless action figures for a horror film, swim caps for a swimming documentary, limited edition books and meditation CDs for a spiritual film are all examples of thinking outside the box and targeting to the niche audiences you are trying to serve.

CHAPTER 14

Teach and They Will Come

One of the most lucrative products an independent film can create is online education. I've been able to leverage every one of my short and feature film projects by creating online courses and workshops. Of course I've taken it to an extreme with my platforms IndieFilmHustle. com, IndieFilmHustle.tv, Filmtrepreneur.com, and BulletproofScreenwriting.tv. You don't have to launch an online film school, podcast, blog, and YouTube channel. Though, you can be very strategic in how you create your product.

Remember Ivan Malekin and Sarah Jayne, the filmmakers behind the feature film *Friends, Foes and Fireworks*? They had a unique value proposition to offer the niche audience of indie filmmakers. They shot the entire feature film in just 24 hours.

I had the pleasure of meeting them at the American Film Market a few years ago and as we sipped some coffee in the lobby they pitched me their film and asked my advice on distribution. During that meeting I said to them, "Have you ever thought of creating an online course teaching filmmakers how to make a feature film in 24 hours?"

Movie poster for Friends, Foes and Fireworks

The thought had never crossed their minds. I explained to them that they had a unique opportunity since there were no other online courses teaching how to make an indie film in 24 hours and they could generate a nice side revenue stream.

They were in. I partnered with them and sold the course on the Udemy platform, more on Udemy in a little bit. Using their existing audience and leveraging my audience the course has generated a nice source of additional revenue for the filmmakers.

The cost to create a course like this is minimal and the returns could be excellent. By partnering with a known brand in the niche space, *Indie Film Hustle*, Ivan and Sarah would be able to jump-start the revenue stream and leave me to do the marketing.

Make sure you capture a ton of behind the scenes footage that cannot only be repurposed for marketing but an online course as well. If you go into producing your film with this in mind you can create amazing course materials live on set. I would suggest you hire someone to just be in charge of recording content for an online course or courses. You will be too busy trying to produce the feature film.

Behind the scenes of Friends, Foes and Fireworks

Creating a course on filmmaking, cinematography, screenwriting, or any part of the filmmaking process is great but there are tons of other opportunities as well.

– CASE STUDY –

Forks Over Knives

The wildly successful documentary *Forks Over Knives* has built an empire off of just one feature film. *Forks Over Knives* is a documentary exploring the health benefits of a plant-based diet. The filmmakers of this film were really ahead of the curve. Being one of the first films on the subject they helped launch the plant-based diet revolution and became a brand that people trusted when it came to plant-based diet information. *Forks Over Knives*, became a brand in itself.

Since the film was released in 2011, the filmmakers have launched multiple ancillary product lines that have generated much more money than just the rental, sale and exploration of the film itself.

A few of the product lines the *Forks Over Knives* producers have launched are: a national magazine, plant-based food line of sauces, frozen food meals, a series of plant-based cookbooks, a recipe app, special edition versions of the documentary, a meal planning service, a thriving YouTube Channel, an informational website and my favorite, a massive series of plant-based cooking courses.

Forks Over Knives partnered with an existing online cooking school to offer a product that is in perfect alignment with their niche audience. If you watch *Forks Over Knives*, decide to make a lifestyle change and want to switch to a plant-based diet you will be looking for educational resources to help you on your journey.

This product fills that need perfectly. The courses are branded with a name the customer already knows and trusts. They come in two packages The Essentials Course (20 hours of videos) at $139.99 and The Ultimate Course (55 hours of videos) at $349.99.

This is also an example of not having to create everything yourself. The *Forks Over Knives* producers decided to partner with a company that had existing content and product line rather than incurring the time and cost of creating something from scratch. This allows the producers to move quickly and present more value to a hungry niche audience, no pun intended.

Forks Over Knives is a perfect Filmtrepreneurial example. If the film-makers would have just gone down the old legacy model of distribution and wouldn't have thought like Filmtrepreneurs, they would have lost hundreds of thousands, if not millions, of dollars in revenue.

WHERE TO HOST YOUR ONLINE COURSES

There are many schools of thought on this subject but here's my take. You could build your own platform using back-end websites like Teachable, Kajabi, and Thinkific or you could decide to host your courses on existing online education platforms like Udemy and Skillshare. There are pluses and minuses to both of these approaches.

If you want to have complete control you could host your courses on your Wordpress website using course creation plugins like Course Cats, LifterLMS, or Zippy Courses. The problem with this approach is that the learning curve can be steep. This is not a beginner's approach.

The cost might be less up front but it will cost you in hosting and traffic charges from your website hosting company, not to mention the technical support issues you will have to deal with as well. The ROI and ROT is not great.

MARKETPLACE PLATFORMS

What are Udemy and Skillshare? These platforms are online education marketplaces. They have millions of potential customers you could sell your online courses to. They also handle the entire back-end for you including hosting, technical support, email support and the ability to receive payments. I know this sounds great. Right? Well, not so fast.

You have very little control over your courses and your customers on these platforms. You have no access to customers' emails, information or analytics. You are playing in someone else's sandbox. Their sandbox, their rules. The revenue splits are also heavily favored toward the platform and not the creator but there are tricks to get around these issues. Let's break down the pros and cons of each platform.

UDEMY

Udemy is one of the largest online educational platforms on the planet. As Udemy states, "Our goal is to disrupt and democratize education by enabling anyone to learn from the world's experts," and they have done just that. The platform allows creators an easy-to-use interface to upload videos, PDF Documents, and PowerPoint Slides all in a simple course experience.

It costs you nothing to upload and host a course on Udemy. The company makes its money by revenue share. Here's how it breaks down, Udemy keeps 50% of all organic sales on the platform, basically if someone goes to Udemy, search and finds your course then 50% goes to you and 50% goes to Udemy. If you drive the sale then you keep 97% of the sale (Udemy takes a 3% transaction fee). The price of courses range from $20 - $200 and you can only price your courses in $5 increments.

I got started on Udemy years ago and I've been very happy with the results. If you accept the rules of this sandbox then you can make a lot of money. You should use Udemy as part of your course's eco-system. It should be one of many revenue streams coming in from your course.

Like I stated before, Udemy does control access to your students, as well as customers' emails, and information. This might be a problem down the line if you want to reach out to your customers with new products that live outside of the Udemy platform.

SKILLSHARE

Skillshare is a great platform to diversify your course's revenue streams. Skillshare provides instructors with tools to create online courses that would be hosted on their platform. Skillshare recommends that courses, or classes as they call them, should run 10-25 minutes in length. The classes should be broken down into short 2-3 minute videos that are pre-recorded and self-paced.

Unlike other platforms, Skillshare is a subscription service. For a monthly fee users obtain access to all the courses on the Skillshare platform. You can't sell individual courses like on Udemy.

Once your class has 25 students, you will be eligible to participate in Skillshare's Partner Program. With the program you can earn money through the royalty pool managed by the company, the instructor generally gets $1-2 per enrollment. As a partner you can create another revenue stream through your teacher referral link. You receive $10 for each new student who signs up on Skillshare through this link.

My experience with Skillshare has been great. The key is volume, the more classes you upload the higher your revenue and the better your ranking is in Skillshare's search. The higher the ranking the more students see your classes. You can create custom classes for the platform or just pull a lesson or two from your $100 course and upload it up onto Skillshare for an extra revenue stream.

COURSE HOSTING PLATFORMS

If you use companies like Teachable, Kajabi and Thinkific then they will handle all the back-end for you. There will be a monthly charge to host your courses on these services, plus most take a small percentage of your sales. In the long term these are excellent choices if you can drive traffic to the courses. These platforms have no audience you can sell to. They are strictly a back-end hosting provider.

TEACHABLE

Being extremely frustrated by Udemy, the Teachable team wanted to create a platform that gave course creators more control and access to their customers. Udemy controls access to your students, as well as customers' emails and information. Teachable enables you to offer online courses "on your website and control your branding, student data, and pricing all from one place."

The best part of Teachable is that you can use it for free and pay $1 + 10% for all transactions. This is a great option for Filmtrepreneurs just starting out. That's what I did. Once I saw revenue start to come in then I jumped to the basic plan which starts at $39 per month ($33.25, if paid annually + a 5% transaction fee).

Unlike other platforms, Teachable's design options are top-notch and they even offer customers the ability to watch courses on an App. That is a major plus. This platform is my chosen way to host many of my courses. If you are creating a high-end course, let's say $100 or more then Teachable is the way to go.

THINKIFIC

Thinkific was around before Teachable and has some good street credibility. This platform provides a truly full-featured software solution for course creators. It can help you create, deliver, market and sell online courses.

The biggest issue I have with Thinkific is its design options. It's limiting for someone like me who loves to control the design of everything I do. With that said, I have colleagues of mine who absolutely love Thinkific so I would try it for yourself.

Just like Teachable, there's a free plan option but unlike other platforms Thinkific doesn't charge transaction fees on any of its plans, paid or free. The Basic Plan starts at $49 per month ($39, if you want to pay it annually). Check it out to see if it works for your course eco-system.

KAJABI

If you already have a website and marketing tools in place then Kajabi might be overkill. As it states on its website "Kajabi is the one system you need to market, sell, and deliver your knowledge online." With Kajabi you will be able to sell not only online courses but memberships, file downloads, training portals, and any other digital product your Filmtrepreneur mind can come up with.

There's something to be said having everything under one roof but all of these features come at a cost. Pricing starts at $149 a month or $119 per month if you go for the annual package. You can start with a 28-day free trial and even jump-start creating your online course by joining Kajabi 28 Day Course Challenge.

I don't recommend this platform for beginners. Kajabi is for the experienced Filmtrepreneurs who have gone down this path before and just want everything under one roof. You need to have a solid product and marketing plan if you plan to spend $149 a month.

COURSE STRATEGY

My strategy is to use all of these methods to get my courses out there. Udemy has a massive customer base, as does Skillshare. Why not have two additional revenue streams from the same course? I also host my courses on Teachable and drive traffic to them directly. I can add special content there and charge more on that platform.

Teachable also allows you to create a membership site where you can charge a monthly or yearly fee to access all of your content. This is great for filmmakers with multiple films, behind the scenes, and courses.

Using a holistic approach to your course creations and distribution, you can generate multiple revenue streams from one product. A word of warning, if you have a course you are selling for $100 on Teachable and you also put that same course for sale on Udemy for $10 your customers will be very upset. My advice is to create different versions of the course for each platform.

CHAPTER 15

Selling Services and Yourself

When I released my short film, *BROKEN* years ago something interesting started to happen. Something that I hadn't planned for at all. Other filmmakers started to reach out to hire me to work on their independent film projects.

My film had so many visual effects on a low budget that filmmakers just didn't want to know how I did it but wanted me to do it for them. The same thing happened with editing and color grading. Every week I would get emails and phone calls asking me what my rate was.

The demand was so high, and thinking like a Filmtrepreneur, I decided to open my own post-production company called *Numb Robot*. Through that company I was able to not only work and make money for myself but I was able to send constant paid work to the amazing visual effects artists who helped me bring *BROKEN* to life.

At the time I was the only post-production company I knew of that was not only catering to independent filmmakers but also using my film projects as the main source of advertising. *Numb Robot* continued to put food on my table years after the release of that little short film. Talk about streams of income.

Look for opportunities to sell your services by using your film project as a calling card. In all the press materials make sure to mention yourself, your company or the service you are trying to sell.

It could be production services, post-production, cinematography, coaching, consulting, online marketing or even services your niche audience would be interested in like a meal prep service inspired by *Crazy, Sexy, Vegan*, search engine optimization, or writing services. Think of a service that your audience needs and fill it.

– CASE STUDY –

Off the Tracks

I had the pleasure of interviewing filmmaker Brad Olsen on my podcast. His Filmtrepreneur story fascinated me. Brad wrote, directed and edited the film *Off the Tracks*, a documentary about the editing software *Final Cut Pro X*.

Movie poster for Off the Tracks

I know, who in their right mind would watch a feature length documentary about editing software? This is as niche of a film project as I had ever come across. *Final Cut Pro X* is an editing software package that was developed by *Apple*.

When *Apple* decided to release the new and revolutionary version of its flagship editing software, people in this community were extremely excited. Unfortunately, Apple's release of the software was easily one of the worst product launches in the history of editing software. The outrage was deafening; even video editors on the *Conan O' Brian Late Night* talk show went on-air and voiced their disgust for the new version.

The subject for the film was going to be polarizing within the community without question. Being an editor myself for over twenty-five years, I know how cultish editors can get about the editing software they use. I knew he would have a passionate audience. Talk about a blue ocean, Brad would have no competition at all in this space.

He created buzz for the project by crowdfunding the film's budget from the community he was going to sell to. The film was unique enough that his story was picked up by every major news outlet in his niche, including *Indie Film Hustle*.

I wanted to find out why he made this film and what his end game was. His answer floored me. Brad's plan was to reach out to industry thought leaders in the editing and post-production space and make a name for himself within his niche. He would not only create revenue streams by self-distributing the feature film on Vimeo, Amazon and Apple TV but he would establish himself as a thought leader in his space.

Brad Olsen editing Off the Tracks

He was able to generate a nice revenue stream from the sales and rentals of the film but more importantly he was able to make invaluable connections in the niche community. He was able to leverage *Off the Tracks* to generate freelancing editing work that would keep the revenue coming for years to come.

After he exhausted the rentals and sales of the documentary, he uploaded a shortened version of the film on YouTube for free to gain an even larger audience for not only the film but for himself and the services he provides. I want you to see that it's not always about making money from the feature film itself, the end game could be getting more work as an editor or selling a service. This is how a Filmtrepreneur thinks outside the traditional box.

CHAPTER 16

Getting Your Film into the World

The legacy distribution system is not designed with the best interests of independent filmmakers in mind. It is designed to keep the pockets of the studios and film distributors full. Don't forget they are a business and are generally designed to protect their own interests first and foremost.

Indie filmmakers have been told that the only way to make money with an independent film is to use a traditional film distributor, or even better, get purchased by a mini or major studio. If you have read this far in the book you know that is not true at all. Most filmmakers have no idea what to do when they get into distribution of their film.

Does a Filmtrepreneur need a traditional distributor? It depends on how you structure the deal. Traditional distributors generally have a large and established network of potential buyers for your film and multiple possible streams of revenue.

The problem is always the deal. Most distribution agreements are set up completely in the favor of the distributor. This makes sense, right? Distribution companies want to make as much money as it can from your product by giving you as little as they legally need to. Some of the agreements I've read are outright robbery.

If you approach a film distributor as if they were your only way to make money from your film project, which is how most filmmakers enter these deals, then you have no leverage at all. But if you approach a film distributor as a Filmtrepreneur and set up the deal as a partnership, which it should be, then you have a much better chance of being successful.

Having a film distributor be part of your larger Filmtrepreneurial strategy can be extremely helpful. If you have a hot film that the distributor knows it can make money with they might offer you an MG or Minimum Guarantee, which is an upfront payment to secure your film paid against future revenue. Don't get too excited about this. MG's are becoming harder and harder to come by.

With the oversaturation of film projects in the marketplace distributors don't have to put out any cash to license films. To get an MG, your film has to be a surefire moneymaker in the eyes of the film distributor. If you are getting this type of offer that is a very good sign. Be warned that many times if you get an MG, that will be the last money you will ever see for your film. Again, it's all how you structure the deal.

There are many benefits with working with a traditional film distribution company. Depending on the distributor you work with they can release your film theatrically, pay for advertising, through their contacts get you cable and paid television deals, DVD and Blu-Ray revenue, streaming offers, and generally get your film project out there in a bigger way than you could do alone.

If you are making the bulk of your money from other revenue streams you have created for your film then a distributor acts like a huge marketing machine that helps you sell your ancillary products. It really all depends on what makes sense for your film project.

With that said there is no reason to sign a bad or predatory distribution deal. Let's go over a few things to help you on your path with a traditional film distributor. Most independent filmmakers suffer heartaches when they deal with traditional film distribution companies because of a few reasons.

- By the time they get to this point in the filmmaking process, they are exhausted.
- Filmmakers are ignorant about the entire process.
- Filmmakers have no idea what to ask for or look out for.
- Many times filmmakers never did market research to see if their

film had any value and when the harsh reality hits them they have very few options, they sign a predator distribution deal to get a digital release of their film.

Not all film distribution companies are immoral or predatory. I've run into many good players in this game, but I've also dealt with some predator distributors that I wouldn't trust to carry my groceries up the stairs.

COMMON FILM DISTRIBUTION MISTAKES

Over the years I've seen a common group of mistakes filmmakers make again and again when using traditional distributors. Here are a few mistakes to avoid.

MISTAKE #1

You see that distributors are calling and e-mailing you because your movie is almost done. They want to see the film before anyone else does. The filmmaker thinks to himself or herself "I'm so special. All these distributors want my movie even before it's done. All I have to do is send out links to all of them and wait for the bidding war to begin." Unfortunately the distribution world doesn't work this way.

Generally if you place your movie in film industry trade magazines like *Variety* or *The Hollywood Reporter* film distributors will put your film on a list and call you when you are almost done. They are hoping to scoop up a good film cheap before the filmmaker has a chance to show the world. Do not make this mistake.

If distributors reach out, keep in contact with them and let them know when you will be having a public premiere at a film festival or an industry screening. Never send a link of your movie to a distributor before the film has screened publicly unless you have a very well established relationship with that distributor.

MISTAKE #2

Your film gets accepted into the Sundance, South by Southwest, Cannes, Tribeca or Toronto Film Festival. All your dreams are about to come true. All you need to do is show up to watch the massive bidding war, collect that fat check from the winning distribution company, and your filmmaking career making $200 million studio films can finally take off.

Not only is this wrong, it's dangerously wrong. When filmmakers get caught up in this "lottery ticket" mentality they are destined for pain and suffering. I speak from experience. Every time I made a short film I was expecting it to catapult my career to the next level like Robert Rodriguez or Quentin Tarantino. Those filmmakers are the exception not the rule.

Hollywood loves to promote these stories because it makes for good press, just like state lotteries show you the winner every week and not the millions of losers who lost their money gambling. Getting into Sundance is not a distribution plan.

I know of many films that won awards at Sundance, SXSW and other top tier film festivals and never sold their films. Getting into these film festivals is not the automatic ATM it was in the early 90's. Does it help to be accepted into one of these big film festivals? Yes. Does it guarantee any? No.

MISTAKE #3

Filmmaker X spends $200,000 to make his film but has no money left in the budget for any marketing. This mistake is insane to me. No other business in the world to my knowledge spends hundreds of thousands of dollars on a product and doesn't budget in money to market the product.

You have to put at least 20% of the budget into the marketing of your film and more if you plan to self-distribute. I include film festival submission fees and travel in this budget. Film festivals is the first wave of marketing many indie films get and most filmmakers do not take advantage of it.

If you don't put money for marketing aside then you are basically hoping for a distribution miracle to happen; a film distributer gives you a huge MG for the rights to your film, an Oscar winning producer sees the film and wants to produce your next film and releases your first film through Warner Brothers where he has an output deal or a high-powered film agent sees it and wants to represent not only the film, but you as well. Do these things happen? Yes. Do they happen often? ABSOLUTELY NOT.

FILM MARKETS

Film markets are where traditional distributors go to sell their catalog of films. I'd like to think of film markets like flea markets but instead of old comic books or antique furniture in a parking lot people are buying and selling movies in a hotel. There are many film markets that take place around the world.

- MIPCOM
- MIPTV
- Cinemart
- NATPE
- European Film Market
- Hong Kong International Film & TV Market (FILMART)
- Hot Docs (For Documentaries)
- Independent Film Week/Project Forum (formerly known as IFP Market)
- TIFFCOM (Content Market at the Tokyo International Film Festival)

The two major film markets in the world are the American Film Market in Los Angeles, California and the Marché du Film or Cannes Film Market in Cannes, France, which is the business counterpart of the Cannes Film Festival.

If you want to learn how films are bought and sold throughout the world you should make a pilgrimage to one of these film markets. Even if you do not have a film to sell it will be an immense educational opportunity. AFM is an eight-day event and generated over one billion dollars in sales of films at every stage of production during that time frame.

As a Filmtrepreneur, film markets are an excellent place for you to network, build relationships with buyers, distribution companies, international sales agents and producers' reps. You can even screen your film there. More on that in chapter 23.

To learn more about how to navigate AFM, I recommend the book, *The Guerilla Rep: American Film Market Distribution Success on No Budget* by Ben Yennie. For more resources on film markets go to www.filmtrepreneur.com/bonus.

EDUCATIONAL RIGHTS

Don't forget to ask for educational rights for your film to be carved out as well. If you want to use behind the scenes footage and clips from your film in an online course product, then you will need educational rights to use the clips; possibly even including the full feature film in the educational product. You need to make sure there is language in the contract that gives you these rights. This is a new concept and completely out of the wheelhouse of a traditional film distributor.

As long as it doesn't impact the distributor's bottom line they should not have an issue with this. Only ask for this if you think you might want to create an online course as part of your Filmtrepreneur strategy.

Another kind of educational rights you should carve out for yourself is the ability to license your film to libraries, universities, museums, schools or similar institutions for exhibition directly to audiences via streaming or closed circuit exhibition. Depending on the topic of your film, the education license could be a major revenue generator. Unless your distributor has some established relationships in this area I would carve these rights out for yourself.

RIGHT TO SELL YOUR FILM

Filmmakers generally never ask potential film distributors where their strengths are. They just sign over all the rights and that's it. I have a secret for you, almost all film distributors, with a few exceptions, are not strong in every part of film distribution.

Most film distribution deals are all inclusive, meaning they take the worldwide rights for your film. Sometimes the film distributor will just want the rights to North America because that's where they have relationships. Some distributors have relationships with Netflix and Hulu; others have strong ties to paid and free cable opportunities.

Many focus on educational and airline rights while others have experience selling overseas. Some are TVOD, AVOD and SVOD experts and others might have deals set up with DVD and Blu-Ray sell-through companies. With my films I have always piecemealed the rights.

You can break up your rights as follows; US rights to one company but Video-On-Demand to another with international rights going to another company. Again it's all how the deal is structured. Many distributors do not like to piecemeal out the rights but see what works for you and your distribution plan. If they want your film bad enough there is always a way to make a deal.

One right I would always fight for is the right to sell your film on your own website. You can sell it via digital download, streaming or DVD/Blu-Ray. By retaining that right you keep the ability to sell your film no matter what happens with the film distributor.

If you know that you want to sell vintage green VHS copies of your horror film then ask for DVD, Blu-Ray and VHS rights. Most distributors will not have an issue with this because it's a revenue stream they generally can't tap into anyway. I'd ask for VHS rights anyway just to see the look on the distributor's faces. Just kidding. Ask them where they have those strengths and carve out those rights to them. You are then free to find another partner that could better exploit those other rights.

Don't think you need to give worldwide rights to just one company for 15 years. You don't. Negotiate and make a deal that makes sense for you and your film. As I hinted before, the film distribution landscape could be very dangerous. Let's take a walk down the dark and dirty back alley of film sales.

CHAPTER 17

The Untold Dark Side of Film Distribution

I despise when filmmakers are taken advantage of and, unfortunately, there's a long history of film distributors doing just that to my filmmaking brethren. I wanted to include this chapter because this is a subject that isn't discussed in public enough. The key to protecting yourself from these predatory film distributors is knowledge.

This is by far the most damaging and dangerous parts of the filmmaking pipeline. A filmmaker can work for years and when they finally get to distribution their film can be stolen right out of their hands if they are not careful.

For the uninitiated, the film distribution world is full of sharks, snakes and thieves. They promise you everything and deliver barely anything. They will present you with the worst contracts just to see if you are ignorant enough to sign it.

Many people have heard the horror stories about an indie filmmaker signing a predatory distribution deal, never getting a dime and losing control of his film for fifteen years to boot. As crazy as that might sound, it happens more often than you might think. These stories are not outliers or exceptions; they are the rule.

Are all distributors predatory? No. There are many good and honest film distributors out there who truly care about independent filmmakers. Can you make money with a traditional distributor? Yes. You just need to understand the rules of engagement. I'll be focusing on the shadowy side of film distribution and will be shining a light into the dark corners of the business where these predators live and work.

If you are going to get taken advantage of by a film distributor there are basically two ways they will do it.

1. The distributor will just lie, cheat, and steal from you on the back-end.
2. The deal you sign is bad from the day you put ink to paper.

Here are a few techniques predatory film distributors use to cheat film-makers.

COOKING THE BOOKS

Most people have heard of the term "Hollywood accounting." This is the practice of opaque or creative accounting methods used by Hollywood when calculating profits from its film projects.

Many times distributors take it a step further and outright falsify sales numbers, expenses and reporting. I've heard of distributors literally adjusting totals in their favor before sending the filmmaker reports, if they send reports at all.

This is not only completely against the law and immoral but these predators take the chance because they know the odds of a filmmaker taking them to court is rare. They assume the filmmaker has little or no resources. If threatened with a lawsuit they might say they made an accounting error and pay you what you are owed.

Hollywood accounting got a lot of media attention years ago when Paramount Pictures reported that the Oscar Winning film *Forrest Gump* hadn't made any money after expenses even though the film grossed $678 million dollars at the box office alone.

OUT OF CONTROL EXPENSES

A gray area all filmmakers need to stay on top of is capping the expenses the film distributor could wrack up in the process of selling your film. Distribution companies usually will charge you for expenses they accrue in the process of distributing your film. Depending on the distributor this could cover trailer editing, poster design, film market travel, final deliverables, close captioning, and many other line items.

The key is to demand a cap on expenses, which means that you are not responsible for any costs above a certain point. Let us say we cap the marketing fees at $20,000. If the expenses are $25,000, then you are only responsible for $20,000. So the first $20,000 made from sales of the film go to covering those expenses.

If you do not request, in very clear language in the agreement, to cap or limit these marketing expenses, then the chances of you ever receiving a dime from the exploitation of your film are extremely slim. Try to provide the distributor with as many deliverable elements as possible.

Line items like poster design, trailer editing, close captioning, and encoding. The more elements you provide for them the better. This way they will not be able to charge you inflated prices for these deliverables.

Charging for deliverables is one way predatory film distributors generate revenue from films even if sales are lackluster. If you see a line item for encoding, unless they do that work in-house they will more than likely farm that work out to a post-production company that will charge them let's say $1500 but they will charge you, the filmmaker, $3000. Not all distributors do this but it's something to be aware of.

THE FILM MARKET CHARGEBACK

When a distributor goes to a film market and represents your film there they will charge every film they are repping, a chargeback fee. If they are billing each film $15,000, which is on the low side, to be at the film market and they are repping let's say 25 films, that's a cool $375,000 in expenses they can chargeback to filmmakers.

And that's if the distributor is only charging 25 films; they could be invoicing many more filmmakers. Most larger distributors can charge filmmakers anywhere between $40,000 to upwards of $100,000 per film for film market expenses if they like.

Just so you understand some cold hard numbers, according to the American Film Market's website it costs as low as $11,000 for one regular office space and a $3500 exhibition fee. Let's also take into account travel, hotel, staff, printing and food expenses for the distributors. We are still nowhere close to $375,000.

For many distributors attending a film market is like spring break in Santa Monica, CA (American Film Market) or Cannes, France (Cannes Film Market). The big bonus is they get to chargeback all the expenses for their trip to the filmmakers and films in their catalog. If you make sure to set up the terms at the beginning there shouldn't be any surprises.

BEWARE OF THE BIG NAME

There are many well-known film distributors out there. Don't be fooled by perception. Just because a distributor has an Oscar winner in one of their films or a title you might have heard of doesn't guarantee they are going to do what they say they are going to do.

There is one film distributor I'm thinking of who has a reputation for being a champion of independent filmmakers but, if you look past the marketing, you'll find out that they are just as predatory, if not more predatory, than some of the smaller companies.

When a film distributor asks for a 15-year-term on an agreement, you need to run away. This company does that all the time and, because of their preserved authority, filmmakers sign on the dotted line and give their film away.

Is every deal they make predatory? No, but they will try to take advantage of filmmakers who are not educated in this world, as most film distributors will. I was speaking to an employee of that company and he told me that there is a poor guy in the office who had to deal with all the angry phone calls from filmmakers who were unhappy about how their film was being handled.

Basically, he stated that the company would sign twenty films and maybe spend money on marketing and promotion for one or two of them. The rest would just get funneled out to all their platforms (Apple TV, Amazon, Google, etc) and that would be it. If no sales came in they would abandon the films and move on to the next month's crop of movies.

The business plan of many of these larger distributors is to acquire as many films as they can and pump those films out onto all the digital platforms and see what sticks. Some of these companies release over 40 new titles every month. That's more than a film a day. How much time, energy and resources do you think they will dedicate to your film? With releasing almost 500 titles a year you can do the math.

Filmmakers would see their films up on all the major platforms and a few would see a DVD of their film on the shelves of Best Buy, Target and Walmart. This doesn't mean you will be getting paid. Many times it's just smoke and mirrors.

Many filmmakers also make the mistake of picking a distributor based on the films they have in their library. I know of many smaller distributors who have lesser-known films in their library but actually pay filmmakers and make them money. Don't be fooled. Don't let your ego handle your distribution decisions.

WORKING WITH A TRADITIONAL DISTRIBUTOR

Here are some essential tips when looking at a potential film distribution partner.

Please note: You should always seek legal counsel who specializes in Entertainment law when deciding to sign any agreement. The information you are about to read is based on my experience being in the film industry for over 25 years and should be a starting point of discussions with legal counsel. Now that we got that out of the way let's get into it.

DO YOUR HOMEWORK

Anytime you speak to a film distributor, always do your homework. Contact filmmakers the distributor has done business with in the past and ask them about their experience. Some questions to ask.

- What did they do for the film?
- Did they pay you?
- Did they pay you on time?
- Did you have to chase them to get paid?
- Were you able to get them on the phone easily?
- How often and detailed are the revenue reports?
- Would you work with them again?

This one tip could save you years of heartaches. I would call at least 5-10 filmmakers and compare notes. You can go to IMDBPro.com (if you don't have an IMDB Pro account get one ASAP) and look up the films the company has distributed before and reach out to the filmmakers of those films. You can find contact information of companies and filmmakers using IMDBPro. See what they have to say; it could help you decide if this film distributor will make a good partner.

HOW LONG HAVE THEY BEEN DOING BUSINESS?

One of the easiest ways to see if the company you are talking to is better than most is to see how long they have been in business. Do they have a track record of paying their filmmakers? This method isn't perfect since I know distributors who have been around for years, who I would never work with, but this does weed out potential problems. The key is doing that homework.

THE DEVIL IS IN THE DETAILS

Now you reached out to a distributor, have done your homework, and you have a beautiful distribution contract sitting on the table for you to sign; all your filmmaking dreams are about to come true. Before you lease that brand-new Tesla, hold on a minute. You need to go over this agreement with a fine-tooth comb.

First, have an entertainment attorney look over the agreement. This is the best investment you can make during this process. Please do not use your Uncle Bob who is a real estate attorney; he will not be savvy enough to understand the little tricks and fine print present in most distribution agreements.

LENGTH OF AGREEMENT

I have seen distribution contracts with terms of 10 years, some even 15 years long. In a nutshell, the distributor owns your film for the length of the agreement. If you have not signed a smart deal with the distributor, then you have basically given your movie away as a gift. Think of it as a donation, but not to a good cause and non-tax deductible. You will not generate any revenue from your hard work, let alone pay back investors, or recoup your expenses.

One-way to hedge your bets on a long-term agreement is to add a performance clause. This states that if the distributor cannot hit certain sales goals by a certain time frame, 18 months is a good starting point, then the film rights revert back to you. If they are promising you sales then have them put their money where their mouth is.

I have signed distribution agreements for as little as three years, not the industry norm. Most arrangements range between 5 to 10 years. Don't forget you can always negotiate the terms. It's your film that you worked hard to create. Never be afraid to ask. So make sure the deal you sign is a good one because you will be in bed with this company for years to come.

CROSS-COLLATERALIZATION

As they say, you always have to read the fine print and cross-collateralization is as fine print as it gets. There are two ways this can be used to make sure filmmakers never get a dime from their film.

The first way is when a film distributor sells your film in a package with other titles. Let's say your film is the hot title a foreign buyer really wants and offers the distributor $10,000 for his territory. That would be great. You should receive a large percentage of that sale. If it was only that straightforward. Not every title the distributor has is a winner so what they do is package your hot film with nine other titles that aren't selling.

The distributor uses your title to help move the other nine titles that no one is willing to pay for. In this new deal the buyer still only pays $10,000 but gets ten titles. Unfortunately, since there are now 10 titles sharing the $10,000 you only get $1000 for your movie, before all the fees and chargebacks of course. You have just been the victim of cross-collateralization.

There is another version of cross-collateralization you need to look out for. Let's say your distributor thinks that your film will do very well on DVD and orders 1000 copies which costs him $10,000. At the same time the distributor places your film on Amazon Prime at no cost. Your film does well on Amazon Prime and generates $9,000 in the first quarter. Unfortunately DVD sales were not as hot and only generate $500.

Someone has to pay for all the DVDs that have been returned from Walmart, and I promise you it won't be the distributor. What they will do is lump in the costs and sales of the DVDs with the revenue your film made from Amazon Prime. With this model your total revenue is $9500 from both DVD and Amazon but your total costs are $10,000 so you are in the hole -$500. You have just been cross-collateralized.

This is one technique that predatory film distributors use to separate you from your money. Make sure that you have very clear language in your agreement with the distributor that does not allow cross-collateralization.

AUDIT RIGHTS

In the agreement, you need to make sure you have the right to audit the distributor's books. I know of a filmmaker who insisted the company put this in the contract and years later that filmmaker went into their office and checked their books.

He discovered thousands of dollars that were owed to him. Most reputable distribution companies will not have an issue with this.

FILMTREPRENEUR POWER MOVE

This tip could save your film from falling into a dark prison that you cannot break it out from. Make sure there is a clause in the agreement that if the distribution company happens to shut down, gets sold, is prosecuted on criminal charges or goes bankrupt, that the rights of your film return to you automatically. Again, most reputable distribution companies will not have an issue with this.

I know Sundance, SXSW and Cannes Film Festival winning filmmakers who had their films locked up in the courts for years because of a bankruptcy. Trust me, you do not want this to happen to you.

See how the game is played? The cards are stacked against the filmmaker as soon as he or she signs on the dotted line. And considering we have been in a buyer's market for independent films, without big stars, indie films are just not selling like they used to at film markets. There is just so much supply that distributors and buyers of films have all the power in this distribution model.

That's why now, and in the future, independent filmmakers will need to look at things differently and think like Filmtrepreneurs. If you can distribute your product directly to the marketplace, control access to your audience, and can cultivate a direct relationship with your niche you will control your own filmmaking destiny.

Hopefully, this chapter has opened your eyes to what could happen if you are not careful. This is why the Filmtrepreneur Method is so important. It allows you to generate revenue from your film without depending solely on a middleman.

CHAPTER 18

Video-on-Demand

VOD or Video-On-Demand can be a confusing term. Is VOD when you rent movies on cable via pay-per-view or is it Netflix or is it when you buy a film on Apple TV? It is all of these. I know you are more confused than before. Let's breakdown each kind of Video-On-Demand.

TVOD

TVOD or Transactional-Video-On-Demand is when you rent or purchase a film or other video content outright on any platform. This could be when you rent the latest Hollywood blockbuster on Amazon or Apple TV and rent another film on Google Play or Fandango. Basically when you pay for access to any film on any platform per film title, that is Transactional-Video-On-Demand.

The question is what platform should you focus on? It all depends. Some filmmakers use a shotgun approach and they put their films on every platform out there. Others focus on one or two platforms at a time to funnel customers and make a larger impact on those platforms.

I recommend focusing on one or two of the major platforms at a time, let's say Apple TV and Amazon, the two biggest platforms. This way you can make an impact on those charts and get access to their massive audience base. The more sales or rentals you have on a platform the higher you will rank on the charts and the higher you rank on the charts the more customers will be introduced to your film organically.

SVOD

SVOD or Subscription-Video-On-Demand is a video service that allows the customer to access an entire video library for a small recurring fee. This fee may be charged daily, weekly, monthly, or annually. Once the customer has paid they can watch as many videos on the service as possible.

The pioneer of SVOD is Netflix. As of 2019 Netflix has over 139 million subscribers worldwide. Other key players in the SVOD space are Amazon Prime Video, Hulu, HBO Now, Starz, Showtime, and CBS All Access just to name a few. Some new juggernauts coming into the SVOD area are NBC/Universal, Warner Brothers, the Walt Disney Company with Disney+, and Apple with Apple TV. The media has coined this "the streaming wars."

Ever since Netflix changed its focus from mail order DVD rentals to an SVOD service, the world of content delivery changed. As I've mentioned, I even threw my hat into the ring by creating the world's first SVOD service dedicated to filmmakers, screenwriters and content creators called *Indie Film Hustle* TV (www.indiefilmhustle.tv).

Filmmakers can license their films to an SVOD outright for a determined length of time. The problem is with the plethora of films in the marketplace many larger SVOD services are becoming extremely picky about the films and series they license and are focusing more of their resources on creating original content that is exclusive on their own SVOD platforms. Think *Stranger Things* and *House of Cards* for Netflix, *Game of Thrones* for HBO or *The Handmade's Tail* for Hulu.

The key to grabbing the big boys' attention is to bring an audience with you. If you, or a star in your film, or the film itself, has a large following then Netflix, Amazon or Hulu would be more inclined to license your film. All of these SVOD services are interested in gaining new customers and if your film or series can do that then you have a very good chance of getting a deal.

SVOD deals generally are for 12-24 months. Some deals are exclusive but many times they are non-exclusive, which means you can license your film to as many SVOD services as you like. Exclusive SVOD deals do not impact your other rights like TVOD, cable, and DVD. It all depends on how you window out your release but each deal is different depending on how much they are paying you upfront.

AVOD

AVOD or Ad-Supported-Video-On-Demand refers to advertising based video on demand and is free to consumers. Much like television, customers need to sit through commercials while watching their favorite shows or movies.

With so many SVOD services in the marketplace many customers are growing tired of spending so much money on SVOD membership fees and are opting to watch for free on AVOD. Since people are used to watching commercials on traditional television and YouTube AVOD has grown in popularity in the past few years.

I know of many Filmtrepreneurs who make more revenue on AVOD than on SVOD and TVOD combined.

PPV

PPV or Pay-Per-View is when a customer requests access to content, generally a feature film or sporting event, to be played at a specific time and place.

The place would be the cable or satellite service provider they are ordering the film through. They would only have access to the content for a predetermined time period.

CHAPTER 19

Self-Distribution

Self-distribution is a buzzword that is on the lips of indie filmmakers around the world. Filmmakers have more direct access to the audience than ever before. Old-world distributors are in decline and the new-world order of self-distribution is the future.

All you have to do is get your indie film up on Apple TV and Amazon, create a few social media posts and watch the money roll in. Unfortunately, it's never as easy as it sounds.

If you have a feature film that cost you $500,000, has a few recognizable actors in the cast and you put it up on Apple TV thinking that your cast will drive all the sales, you will be sorely disappointed.

By now you should know I'm a big supporter of DIY (Do It Yourself) filmmaking, of out of the box thinking, and creating disruptive distribution models. This is what being a Filmtrepreneur is all about. With that said, not every film is a good candidate for self-distribution.

In the past, filmmakers had no way to sell their films directly to the consumer on a mass scale. They had no choice but to go through a traditional film distributor. With the advent of the Internet the doors of film distribution have been blown open.

With all this new access comes a crushing amount of competition. Technology has also made making a high quality feature film easier than ever before. The marketplace is oversaturated and consumers have too many choices for their entertainment.

The essential skill that filmmakers and Filmtrepreneurs need in the new world of indie filmmaking is the ability to spread awareness and market their films. Without a clear understanding of marketing, social media, audience building, and crowdsourcing your film has very little chance of rising above the noise of the crowded marketplace.

For a film to have a successful self-distribution run a few things need to be in place.

1. The film needs to be developed with a niche audience in mind.
2. The filmmakers should have a niche audience that they can reach or have already cultivated.
3. The filmmakers need to do market research in order to test the viability of the project for that niche audience.
4. The cast should have a decent if not large social media presence and be willing to leverage their audiences to help bring awareness to the film.
5. When casting, filmmakers need to hire at least one or two actors with a large social media following and/or name recognition in the niche they are trying to target.
6. The filmmakers need to determine what budget range the niche audience they are targeting can support.
7. The filmmakers should also investigate secondary, tertiary, and fourth place niche audiences the film may appeal to.
8. The filmmakers should have a marketing campaign strategy in place, including social media, traditional and/or grass roots.
9. The filmmakers need to have a distribution windowing strategy in place.
10. The filmmakers should have some strategic partnerships in place with companies, websites, news outlets or influencers in the niche audience's space.
11. The budget of the film should be below $250,000 and 25% of that budget should be allocated to paid marketing.
12. The filmmakers need to allot 8-12 months, if not more, for the entire self-distribution run of the film.

The larger the budget the more money you'll need to generate to get the film into the black and the more savvy and experienced the filmmaker needs to be to make a dent in the marketplace.

Films with budgets over $250,000 that make a profit that solely uses a self-distribution model is extremely rare. Does it happen? Absolutely. I have presented multiple case studies in this book that illustrates that but all of those case studies had many, if not all, of my self-distribution guidelines checked.

DISTRIBUTION WINDOWING

The major studios have been in an ongoing battle with movie theater owners for years over distribution windowing. Windowing is the time allotted to segment the release of a feature film on multiple platforms and media.

Studios want to release their blockbuster films on DVD/Blu-Ray and VOD closer to the theatrical release date of their films. This makes perfect sense from the movie studio's perspective. They spend hundreds of millions of dollars marketing a film and 120 days after the release the audience has forgotten the film even exists.

Theater owners want to make that window longer so more moviegoers come to the theater because of the exclusivity and, of course, to buy more popcorn, sodas, and candy, their high profit margin products. Fewer moviegoers, fewer profits. Why would I rush out to a movie theater, pay for babysitting and spend upwards of $80 for tickets, popcorn and soda when I can watch it on Apple TV in 30 days?

As a Filmtrepreneur you need to have a windowing strategy for the release of your film; if you don't you could cannibalize your sales and leave money on the table.

Let's lay out a basic release window strategy for an indie feature film in North America.

- Theatrical
- On-Demand & Community Screenings
- DVD/Blu-Ray - 30 day Window (only available on film's website)
- DVD/Blu-Ray - Mass release same time as TVOD
- TVOD/Satellite and Cable Television - 90 day Window
- Educational/Library/Airline Release - Same Window as TVOD

- SVOD - Netflix - 1 year Window
- AVOD - Tubi TV, Pluto TV (Last release window)

This is an example of a typical release schedule. During this time you can also be selling rights to your film internationally to different territories.

– CASE STUDY –

This is Meg

When I set out to direct my first feature film, *This is Meg*, I knew right away I would be self-distributing it. I decided that the entire project would be designed from the start to challenge me in ways I had never been before. Not only did I direct the film but I was also the cinematographer, camera operator, editor, colorist, post and visual effects supervisor, trailer editor, marketer, social media manager and head of crowdfunding. I'm sure I missed a few other positions but you get the idea.

I wanted *This is Meg* to be a case study for the *Indie Film Hustle* Tribe. I wanted to have a homegrown example that the Filmtrepreneur Method could not only work but inspire others to do the same.

Crowdfunding had been a foreign concept to me until I started the development of *This is Meg*. I decided that I would go through the process of crowdfunding as not only a learning experience for me but to report back to my community. I ended up going with the crowdfunding platform Seed and Spark. We ended up raising little over $15,000 in cash and donations. Since the budget was so low I was already shooting the movie before we launched the campaign.

We used that money to pay for the budget but to also cover film festival travel costs, marketing and film deliverables like the DCP (Digital Cinema Package), close captioning and mastering.

My marketing strategy was simple, I would leverage my audience and the audiences of the amazing cast I was working with to get the word out. It would be grass roots. Considering that I was already in the black any money that would come in was pure profit. This is one of the benefits of keeping your costs low and lean.

Now how and where to release the film. We world premiered at the

Cinequest Film Festival and had a very nice festival run. As that was going on, I was working behind the scenes to get the VOD release ready. I used a film aggregator to place *This is Meg* on iTunes, Amazon, Google Play, and multiple other streaming platforms.

A film aggregator is a company that, for an upfront cost, places your film on multiple digital VOD platforms. Typically VOD platforms won't accept films from individuals so you need to use a film aggregator. These aggregators provide other services like getting your film encoded, quality control, and other film deliverable elements.

One of the benefits of going through a film aggregator is you usually keep 100% of the revenue generated from the platforms you are placed on, minus any splits from the platforms themselves. Each company is different so do your homework.

The film aggregator was not only able to submit *This is Meg* to the major TVOD platforms but they also submitted the film to the SVOD giant Hulu. The film was licensed to Hulu for a year, which generated a nice revenue stream.

Before you jump into self-distribution you need to do some hard math. Could the revenue you generate from a specific platform, let's say Apple TV, justify the cost of submitting through an aggregator? If you spend $10,000 to get your film on every platform you really need to figure out what your ROI will be. Do your research and see what platforms you think your film will do the best on. The three I always recommend are Amazon, Apple TV, and Google Play for SVOD and TVOD.

You should also release your film on one platform at a time so you can focus your audience to buy or rent there. The more sales you can push on a given platform the higher you will climb on the charts and you'll have a better chance of being found organically.

We launched *This is Meg* on iTunes and Amazon first then slowly released it on other platforms. Sales went very well and still continue to this day. I eventually released it on *Indie Film Hustle TV* as part of the subscription and it is one of the most watched films on the platform.

I continued to monetize the film through podcasts laying out the blueprint on how we made it. I created articles for my blog IndieFilm-Hustle.com detailing the film gear I used in the making of the film, then added affiliate links to those products to generate passive income and adding behind the scenes footage to IFHTV. More on affiliate marketing later in the book. These are just a few methods I used to create revenue streams from a small $5000 budget indie film.

Always thinking like a Filmtrepreneur I decided to partner with a traditional distribution company to sell the international rights to *This is Meg*, an area I had no way of exploiting. I carved out SVOD and TVOD but the rest of the rights were available. The film was sold to multiple territories overseas, again generating additional revenue that I hadn't anticipated.

Overall *This is Meg* was a remarkable success. Could I retire from the proceeds generated? No. Was the film profitable and made much more than its budget? Yes. Will the film continue to generate revenue for me in the years to come? Absolutely!

Filmtrepreneurs don't look at a feature film as a lottery ticket, they look at a film as a product in their portfolio. The more products the better. As you build a library of film projects and revenue streams you will soon realize that the balance in your bank account keeps growing and growing.

FROM DSLR TO $500,000

Let's take a look at an example of self-distribution done right. In chapter 12, I introduced you to Michael and Mark Polish, the filmmakers behind the no budget feature film *For Lovers Only*. What makes their filmmaking story so interesting is how their film generated over $500,000 through self-distribution on iTunes. How might you ask? By thinking like Filmtrepreneurs, leveraging existing niche audiences, and using social media to sell their film.

The brothers were extremely savvy when they cast Stana Katic, not only for her amazing beauty and talent but because she also had a huge fan base from her hit ABC television show *Castle*. At the brothers' request, Stana tweeted out to her over 67,000 twitter followers that the film was available on iTunes and word spread very quickly.

The brothers leveraged not only their own social networks but also Stana's. Her rabid Twitter and Facebook followings spread the word like wildfire. Then the brothers found that the film's #hashtag was drawing over 1,000 tweets an hour, they drafted up movie posters using the Twitter raves in place of critics' quotes. Those movie posters went viral on Twitter and Tumblr, and further helped create an amazing amount of iTunes pre-sales.

I can't express to you enough that they created this film completely in the DIY, no budget filmmaking process. From shooting it to marketing and selling it they were always thinking like Filmtrepreneurs.

Once the film had run its self-distribution course they decided to partner with a traditional film distributor to begin the second life for the film. Since then *For Lovers Only* has been sold around the world and keeps generating a passive revenue stream for the brothers. For a deeper dive into the making of *For Lovers Only*, you can listen to my inspirational interviews with Michael and Mark Polish by going to www.filmtrepreneur.com/bonus.

CHAPTER 20

Film Aggregators – A Warning

As I mentioned earlier, film aggregators are companies you can pay to get your film up on the major TVOD, SVOD and AVOD platforms. These companies have been marketed as saviors that will save you from the big bad predatory film distributors. Can they help you gain access to big platforms you would never be able to submit to? Yes. But you need to follow many of the same rules I laid out for traditional distributors.

ACCOUNTING AND ACCESS

Just like a traditional distributor, aggregators need to provide you with reporting and payment from sales of your film. I know many filmmakers who used a popular, and now closed down, film aggregator, and had an impossible time trying to not only get reporting but also getting paid the money they were owed. The phone number on their website was just an answering machine that would direct them back to the website. They couldn't get anyone on the phone.

Their emails were ignored. It was a nightmare because they needed that aggregator to pull their films off the SVOD platforms so they could go with another aggregator or distributor. Amazon and Apple would not pull down films from their platforms based on the filmmaker's word.

You need to do your research and make sure the film aggregator you choose will be accessible by phone and email. I would see how fast you can get someone on the phone and via email before you make your decision.

Make sure they have an online portal you can log into to see your revenue, and has an easy payment system. Do your research. Call film-makers who have used them before and see what kind of experience they had. Look the film aggregator up online and see if you find any red flags or damning reviews. Do your research and make an educated decision.

WHERE'S MY MONEY?

When speaking to a potential film aggregator ask them if the money your film generates on the platforms goes into a general operational bank account or if the money is deposited into an escrow or separate account. If they don't have an escrow account the operational monies and film-maker's payments are commingling. This is not a good thing. There are potential chances for problems here.

If the company is mismanaged or it doesn't handle its finances well there could be an issue if the money that is owed to you lives in the same accounts that the company pays bills, salaries and other expenses out of. You don't think it can happen? Think again. For more information about potential problems with film aggregators go to www.filmtrepreneur.com/bonus.

WHAT DO YOU MEAN I LOST MY REVIEWS?

When you sign with an aggregator they place your film on the major platforms like Apple TV and Amazon. As the months and years go by you begin to gain ratings and reviews for your film on those platforms.

If, for whatever reason, you want to pull your film off of the plat-forms because you want to sell the rights to your film to a traditional distributor or move to another aggregator you can potentially lose all of those reviews and ratings. You would need to start from scratch again. Though I have heard of films keeping their ratings on some platforms if you reach out to them and request it. Something to be aware of.

YOUR BROKEN NETFLIX DREAMS

The distribution world is in constant flux. Platforms are changing business models faster than filmmakers can adapt. At one time Netflix, Amazon and Hulu were licensing a ton of independent content and paying top dollar. Those days are gone.

All the major streaming services realized it would make more business sense to develop and produce their own content. This way they own the rights for life and don't have to worry about licensing outside content.

Is Netflix still buying outside content? Yes. Are they paying top dollar? No. Netflix, along with all the other streaming platforms, want more subscribers. If you have a film with a big star your chances are better. If you have a stand-up comic with 3 million followers in your film Netflix will not only buy your project but will probably develop an original show around the comic, you, as well.

SVOD for indie filmmakers is drying up fast. Understanding how to create revenue from other distribution sources is more important than ever. My next case study is a perfect example of that.

CHAPTER 21

Four Walling

Four walling is the process of renting or booking a theater for a public screening of your film. Essentially, you contact a movie theater or venue and ask the rate to rent the screen for a certain amount of time. Sometimes the theater will charge you per time slot, per day or per week.

Every movie theater chain is different. If a movie theater has 24 screens and you can generate more money for them on a Thursday night than a studio blockbuster's sixth week in release then they'll be more than happy to sell you that screen for the determined time.

Here's where it gets sticky. As a Filmtrepreneur, you need to understand the economics and risks associated with four walling. If you rent a screen for one week for $10,000 then you need to sell more than $10,000 in tickets for this to make sense. I know that sounds simplistic but you would be surprised how many filmmakers don't even take this into consideration. But if you know you can fill those screenings then you can generate a nice amount of revenue.

Many filmmakers are just so excited to see their film play on the same screen that played the latest Oscar winner that their eyes just glaze over and they forget all about the business. They overestimate their own ability to fill the screening and underestimate the time and cost it will take to put butts into seats.

If you are going to four wall your film, identify eight to twelve key cities that have the most concentration of your core niche audience. Then target that audience by using Google or Facebook ads. Before you even get to that point in the process you should have already been creating buzz and awareness in those markets.

Four walling can be a very expensive gamble but it can also pay off beautifully if done correctly. The next case study illustrates how four walling can really pay off.

– CASE STUDY –

Awake - The Life of Yoganada

Filmmakers Paola di Florio & Peter Rader were part of the team that created the documentary *Awake: The Life of Yogananda*. The film is an unconventional biography about the Hindu Swami who brought meditation and yoga to the West in the 1920s. Paramahansa Yogananda was the author of the spiritual classic *Autobiography of a Yogi*, which has sold over 30 million copies worldwide and is a go-to book for spiritual seekers, philosophers, and yoga enthusiasts today. Apparently, it was the only book that Steve Jobs had on his iPad at the time of his death.

Peter and Paola understood that they had a special film with a massive built-in audience. *Awake* was the perfect candidate for a Hybrid Distribution Model. The term "Hybrid distribution" was coined by filmmaker and consultant Peter Broderick. Hybrid distribution is a combination of direct sales by filmmakers (e.g. theatrical, community screenings, four walling) with traditional distribution by third party companies (e.g. traditional cable and television channels, SVOD, TVOD, AVOD companies, DVD/Blu-Ray distributors, educational distributors).

They started to create buzz for the film by attending conferences where their niche audience would be attending. They handed out free copies of *Autobiography of a Yogi* with a postcard of their film inside. They attended Yoga conferences and approached celebrity yoga instructors about spreading the word to their followers, leveraging influencers in their niche space. Considering there were no other documentaries on Yogananda's life there was no competition. They were most definitely in a blue ocean.

They decided to four wall a theatrical run and targeted a handful of cities where there was a high concentration of Yogananda's followers. They started in New York where they booked a screen for one week for $10,000. Because they had been using social media to get the word out and used strategic partnerships they were able to sell out that entire week, generating $34,000 in gross ticket sales.

The theater was so impressed by the sales, they booked the film traditionally for an additional six week run. Same thing happened in Los Angeles and in a few other markets. Attendance was so high in Los Angeles that the film kept playing for twenty-three weeks at the Laemmle Theater in Pasadena, CA.

After the word got out on the numbers they were pulling in New York, other theater chains started contacting the filmmakers to book *Awake* on their screens. The film ended up screening in sixty-five markets theatrically around the United States. Internationally was no different. In seven countries *Awake* played in over fifty theaters.

Peter and Paola also created community screenings at yoga studios, churches, and schools. They would license DVDs at a higher price point for use in these community screenings. The great thing about using disruptive distribution methods is the ability for the filmmakers to control their customers' data. They had emails from all of their customers, which they used to sell ancillary products from the film down the line. The theatrical and community screenings went on for almost a year.

With all the noise they were making in theaters Netflix came calling. Peter and Paola decided to hold off on licensing to Netflix while they were in theaters. That strategy worked. By the end of the negotiations Netflix quadrupled their offer for the film and agreed to allow them to release the film first on DVD, then TVOD and finally on Netflix.

Peter and Paola made a deal with a traditional distributor for brick and mortar DVD distribution but carved out the right to sell their own DVDs as well. They created a one-month window where customers could only buy the film's DVD through them, then the distributor would be able to do a wide release.

They partnered with the *Self-Realization Fellowship*, an organization that Yogananda founded to create ancillary products like a companion book and original soundtrack they sold along with the DVD. To watch the interview with Peter and Paola go to www.filmtrepreneur.com/bonus.

CHAPTER 22

On-Demand Screenings

Filmmaker Antonio Pantija took the idea of four walling to an entirely new level with his micro-budget horror feature *One Must Fall*, a horror-comedy slasher set in the 80's about a woman wrongfully fired from her office job and forced to take on a temporary job on a crime scene cleanup crew.

Many industry professionals warned him not to pay for a public screening of *One Must Fall* in his home town of Louisville, Kentucky. The traditional wisdom was that nobody would show up to watch a local micro-budget indie horror film in a theater, without a major marketing budget to support the screening.

Movie poster for One Must Fall

Antonio didn't have any money for marketing but what he did have was a niche audience he had been cultivating for over a year. The audience had been taken on the journey of making *One Must Fall* and when the opportunity came up to finally watch it he had no trouble filling the theater.

Packing the house for the event screening of One Must Fall

Always thinking like a Filmtrepreneur, Antonio decided to turn the screening into a major event in town. He decorated the theater in the theme of his creepy film. It was almost like walking into an indoor horror amusement park. He set up some scenes from his film in the lobby so guests could walk around the mini-sets and take pictures with roaming creepy characters he hired to walk around and scare the theatergoers. All these images and videos were posted on social media sites further promoting his film.

He ended up selling over 1050 tickets at $15 and 150 VIP tickets at $100, which included high-end appetizers, free alcohol, reserved seating and a swag bag with tons of stuff from the sponsors. Yes, Antonio had sponsors for his local hometown screening that helped to cover the cost of renting the historical theater they held the event at.

Press interviewing director Antonio Pantija

Antonio made a massive amount of revenue in one evening and the sales didn't stop there. Understanding that he had a very engaged customer base at the screening, he set up a booth selling *One Must Fall* merchandise and took in an additional $5000 in sales.

If you are going to four wall your film you should design the screening into an event. If you are in a big city like New York or Los Angeles it could be a bit more challenging but still doable. The competition is fierce for entertainment dollars. It is easier to create that event screening in a smaller market.

You can more easily receive media coverage in those markets and really get the word out on the screening. Never underestimate people's fascination with Hollywood and filmmaking, especially if they've never been exposed to a red carpet event screening.

Before my long festival run for my short film *BROKEN*, my producer and I set up a four wall screening at a local theater in Miami, FL and made it into an event. We sold out two screenings of our short film and were off and running on a road to an extremely profitable short film.

ON-DEMAND COMMUNITY SCREENINGS

Many filmmakers think that a theatrical run of their indie films is a pipe dream and could never happen. In today's world there are multiple companies that can help you with a theatrical release of your film with little or no money up front. Companies like Tugg.com have been helping filmmakers do just that.

If you are willing to put in the time and hustle, an on-demand self-distributed theatrical run of a film can not only generate revenue but can be a launching ground for you to sell other products and services. According to Tugg's website this is how it works.

Step 1: Fill out the Event Request Form to pick the film, date, time, and place for your screening.

Step 2: The theater approves the request, and you can begin selling tickets on your personalized Event Page.

Step 3: Sell enough tickets before the event deadline to confirm your screening. If you don't meet this "threshold," no one will be charged and your event will be called off.

Step 4: Sit back and enjoy the movie with your community!

The film *Touch the Wall* is a remarkable success story of what can be done when you make a film that caters to a specific niche audience. The film is about swimming phenom and Olympic Gold Medalist Missy

Franklin and how veteran Kara Lynn Joyce helped Missy on her journey to greatness. The producers decided that an on-demand self-distribution model would be the best way to reach their niche audience, which was anyone interested in the sport of swimming.

They partnered with USA Swimming, which allows the producers access to local swim teams across the country. They began to set up screenings everywhere they could. They were able to bring together over 450 K-12 swim teams and each community helped getting the word out about the screenings.

In total they hosted over 360 theatrical screenings, were in theaters for nearly a year, had over 56,400 people attend the screenings and generated over $765,000 in gross revenue making it one of the most profitable on-demand feature films in history.

Because the producers decided to self-distribute through Tugg they had emails from all the people who attended their screenings. They had a huge email list they reached out to when they released the film on DVD, Blu-Ray and VOD.

Being true Filmtrepreneurs, the producers also created multiple ancillary products designed specifically for their niche audience. They sold products like official movie posters, t-shirts, hats, silicone swim caps, special edition DVD and Blu-Rays with a 32 page hardcover book and premium bundles of these products. They also sold over 125+ non-theatrical licenses for the film and also sold educational licenses for K-12 and colleges.

By thinking like a Filmtrepreneur these filmmakers were able to self-distribute their documentary to a niche audience that was dying to see their film. Then they were able to leverage that on-demand theatrical run to create other revenue streams from online sales and ancillary product lines.

SELLING YOUR FILM AT
EVENTS AND CONVENTIONS

An outlet that many filmmakers don't even consider when trying to sell their films is events and conventions. The concept is still the same, go to where your audience lives and hangs out to sell them the product that is designed for them.

If you have a plant-based food documentary wouldn't it make sense to go to a vegan or mindfulness convention? If you have a horror film wouldn't it make sense to rent a table at the many horror conventions around the country and sell your wares? That's exactly what I did with my film *BROKEN*.

My short had a very creepy vibe and the horror audience really dug it. This was a niche audience I didn't anticipate but when I discovered I had a new crop of customers I figured out where they hung out and went there to sell my film.

Setting up our booth to sell BROKEN DVDs and merchandise

I would offer the promoter a free screening of my film at the horror convention in exchange for a cheaper table price. I sold tons of DVDs and original artwork from the short and the feature film version we were planning. I had some of the actors from the film come out in costume to sign autographs and take pictures.

Customers purchasing BROKEN merchandise

I also went to comic book conventions and did the same thing. I would set up a television in my booth and run the trailer for the film on loop. This would bring the audience to our table where I would close the deal. I would sell limited edition artwork at each convention that was tailored to the audience. This method does take work and time but can be extremely fruitful.

CHAPTER 23

Selling Your Film Yourself at a Film Market

Depending on your film project going directly and trying to sell your film at a film market might be a great option. Jonathan Wolf, the managing director of the American Film Market says "Film festivals are cultural events for the community. Don't take your film to a festival." I couldn't agree more. For certain kinds of movies film festivals make sense but for others going directly to film markets could be a better solution.

If your film is an action adventure with a known star, a thriller with a recognized female actress, horror or family film with animals and cute kids then you should take your film to a film market. There are other niche genres like faith-based, urban and animation that do well but the more niche you go at a film market the harder it is to sell the film.

There are over 5000 film festivals around the world and over 50 just in Los Angeles alone. Film festivals are curated and film programmers pick the art they want to screen. Business, at least on the filmmaker's side, is nonexistent. Film markets are all about the business, they do not care about the art. Why not pay to screen your film at a film market?

The film market you should attend if you live in North America is the AFM, the American Film Market and if you are on the other side of the world you could attend either the Marché du Film that coincides with the Cannes Film Festival or the European Film Market that coincides with the Berlin Film Festival. Most buyers go to all the markets so there is really no reason to travel to all of them unless you really want to.

The main purpose of you screening your film at a film market is not to attract a traditional distribution company, though you may want to entertain offers if they make good business sense. The end game of screening at a film market is to sell your film to film buyers.

You are looking to sell your film to international buyers and possibly selling off certain rights like pay cable, television, cruise ships, libraries, and airlines. You are in control and you get 100% of the sale. This also should not interfere with your other Filmtrepreneur revenue streams. It all depends on the end goals you have for your film project.

I'll focus on the American Film Market for this example. The AFM will generate over $1 billion in business over the eight-day event from over 8000 industry marketgoers from 80 countries. The AFM transforms the Santa Monica Promenade and the surrounding community into AFM screening rooms. They will screen over 700 films on 29 screens in the course of the market.

How much does it cost to screen your feature film at the AFM? Generally anywhere from $200 to $400 for AFM on-demand screenings and $1000 to $1700 for a higher-end screening environment. Remember AFM is not a film festival, it is an actual marketplace with buyers attending. Film festival submission fees run anywhere from $50 - $120 with little or no buyers.

This sounds great, where do I sign up? Not so fast, there's a catch. Only exhibitors who have paid the exhibition conference pass can screen their films at the market, if they pay an additional fee. If your film is not represented by an exhibitor already in AFM how can a filmmaker screen their film? According to AFM'S website, "You may contact one of the exhibiting sales companies for representation. The AFM will not recommend any specific exhibitor nor is it involved in these arrangements. You can choose from a list of sales companies that are IFTA (Independent Film & Television Alliance) members."

Many of these companies might do a pay to play deal where you pay them a fee so you can use their exhibition conference pass to screen your film. This may be a more affordable option.

If, after you have done your market research and believe you have a film that could sell at the AFM then it's really simple, you can just pay the fees and screen your film. As I mentioned before, the exhibition fee is $3500 and the exhibition space is $11,000. I know what you are thinking, that's a lot of money for an indie filmmaker. There is always a way to make it happen.

You can partner with a distribution company to share the costs of the exhibition space and the bonus of doing this is that you'll be able to take advantage of the traffic coming through the door. Many film distributors share spaces to keep the costs down.

Another option is to partner with other filmmakers to share in the costs. I suggest you check with whichever film market you may want to screen your film at to see what the current prices and rules are. If you want a list of contact information for every major film market go to www. filmtrepreneur.com/bonus.

Most filmmakers do not know that screening their indie project at a film market is even an option. They submit to Sundance and pray that their film wins that lottery. Remember going down this road is not for every kind of film. If you know that your production value is not up to par or your film is an art house kind of project, screening at a film market should not be part of your distribution plan.

CHAPTER 24

Regional Cinema Model

We've been discussing finding your niche audience and creating films or products for that audience. Filmmaker Daedalus Howell has taken this concept to another level by creating a film that is targeted to his local community. His arthouse sci-fi dramedy *Pill Head* was designed for his small hometown Merced, California which is just outside of San Francisco.

Daedalus knew that an arthouse or an "art-ploitation" film as he calls it would do well in this area full of art film lovers, if done for a price. He was able to produce the film for a $30,000 budget. Most of the financing was made up from crowdfunding and local donations, so he only paid $8000 out of pocket to produce the film.

He was able to galvanize the town to help him bring his film to life. From discounted permits to getting permissions from all the merchants in town, Daedalus was hustling. To release the film theatrically he convinced a consortium of local exhibitors that he would be able to pack the screenings if they would book the film. This meant he didn't have to four wall his film or create an on-demand screening.

The theater exhibitors agreed and this small indie ended up on multiple screens, not only around his hometown but in nearby towns as well. Daedalus' micro-budget film would be playing next to Hollywood's latest blockbusters. *Pill Head* went on to generate well over the $8000 they needed to break even. This, before they ever released the film online.

Always the Filmtrepreneur, Daedalus also created ancillary products like t-shirts and poster prints that generate a steady stream of income every month. His plan is to continue to make locally driven future films and build a portfolio of projects that will be generating revenue for his company for years to come.

What I love about the regional cinema model is that you are definitely in a blue ocean. There is little or no competition. If you are able to produce a film at a low budget you can be very successful with this distribution model. And the best part is that once the film makes its rounds locally you still have the opportunity for other audiences to find it on Amazon, Apple TV or other online platforms. This regional cinema model works almost anywhere in the world, as you will soon see.

– CASE STUDY –

Wakaliwood

Imagine you were back in the early 1900's, when the film industry was a newborn. People were learning and experimenting with the revolutionary technology of moving pictures. Craftsmen were excited about discovering new ways of creating art with this powerful and amazing new technology. You'd think that could never be recreated in today's high tech world but you would be mistaken.

Self-taught filmmaker and serial Filmtrepreneur Isaac Nabwana has almost single handily created the Ugandan film industry without having any filmmaking knowledge or current technology. Isaac is easily one of the most passionate filmmakers I've ever met. Without all the opportunities and technology we in the United States take for granted, he created an entire film industry with literally string and tape.

Using the regional cinema model, Isaac and the committed team from his production company Ramon Film Productions, have created over 40 feature films in the past nine years. Their most popular and successful film being *Who Killed Captain Alex*. Their passion oozes out of their films in a way you couldn't manufacture even if you tried.

In Uganda, where working artists are extremely rare, Isaac has taken the brave step to make a living from his passion. His filmmaking business supports not only his family but his entire community. His ability to perform market research, produce a film product, market and sell that product to his niche audience has been his life's blood.

When you watch Isaac's movies you see a strong influence of 80's action films, Chuck Norris and Chinese kung fu cinema. His favorite film is the 80's classic action film Commando starring the legendary Arnold Schwarzenegger. Isaac focuses on the action genre and bases the storylines of his films on life in Uganda, with an entertaining twist that is specific to his niche audience.

Understanding his marketplace and providing value to his audience is what made Isaac's films so popular. Ever since he started posting clips and behind the scenes videos on YouTube, Isaac's work has garnered a rabid fanbase around the world. This is a spillover audience that he had never intended to sell his films to. Let's breakdown each part of his process.

BUDGET

Isaac keeps the budgets of his movies low, really low by western standards, about $200 US per project. By keeping the budgets so low he's able to make a profit on each of his films.

PRODUCTION

The Wakaliwood team uses the village as a backlot for all of their films. Each day of production they are redressing locations that have already been shot. Isaac has used his backyard as one of the main outdoor sound stages. They have a green screen nailed to the side of a wall for the visual effects shots.

At the studios they have makeshift rehearsal rooms, a makeup room, and prop departments. Professional film equipment is extremely hard to come by, but in the Ugandan villages anything is possible. As they say "Use what you have," and they do just that.

Wakaliwood's prop master, who is a mechanic by trade and one of their leading actors, uses scrap metal to build their heavy weapons. Bullets are hand carved from wood and strapped onto the newly built prop machine guns.

The prop master also designs and develops camera gear including dollies, cranes, and even our 16' jib camera crane that works amazingly well for being built from spare car parts. They even built a life-size helicopter frame which isn't finished yet but that doesn't stop them from using it in their productions.

POST-PRODUCTION

Isaac builds his computers from whatever used and scrap parts he can conjure up. His computer systems last two or three months at best, eventually falling victim to heat, dust, and power surges.

At the beginning he taught himself Adobe Premiere 1.5 for editing and Adobe After Effects for visual effects by reading the help files. There was no Internet in his village when he started on his filmmaking journey, so no YouTube tutorials for him. Isaac's special effects have earned him the reputation in Uganda of being a powerful witch doctor – even by the local police, who still do not understand how he can make a bullet come flying out of a wooden gun.

Isaac is constantly educating himself on the filmmaking process. He devours online courses, YouTube tutorials and any other information he gets his hands on. He also teaches what he has learned to young children in the village. He says he does this for three reasons. By teaching his filmmaking process to the next generation he gives them job skills, he's built up his future workforce and he is creating future customers for his product. You can't get more Filmtrepreneur than that.

DISTRIBUTION

Theatrical Screenings: A Ugandan movie theater, or video hall, typically has two television screens: one for a football game, with the sound turned off, and the other for the feature presentation. In lieu of subtitles, the VJ or Video Joker provides the necessary exposition so the audience can better understand the movie.

A "Video Joker" is a live narrator who can best be described as a cross between an enthusiastic cheerleader, stand-up comedian, and slum tour guide. The joke was that VJ's didn't know the story either and just made it up – and a comedy act was born. Isaac screens his films at these video halls and takes a percentage of the ticket sales.

DVD and Blu-Ray: There are no film distributors in Uganda so Isaac and his team must sell and market their films themselves, selling door-to-door in and around the slums of Kampala, with the occasional road trip to larger towns when money is available.

When a film is ready for distribution Isaac and his family have used DVD burners to master, label, and package the DVDs at home, when electricity is available. Copies are sold for 2500 UGX (about 90 cents US). Half goes to the actors who do the selling, yes the actors are the sales force and the remainder goes back to Wakaliwood.

DVD Distribution expenses are as follows:

- Blank DVD   500 UGX
- Electricity   100 UGX
- Label   100 UGX
- Artwork   80 UGX
- Packaging   40 UGX

This leaves approximately 400 UGX (14 cents US) for Isaac, his family, and Wakaliwood. The number is even lower when costs for transport and spoilage are factored in. Spoilage is when DVDs won't play, or are damaged due to power fluctuations during the burning process.

He now sells his DVDs to a worldwide audience and has even secured an international distribution deal for two of his most popular titles, Who Killed Captain Alex and Bad Black.

SALES FORCE

Like I mentioned before, the Wakaliwood actors are the sales force for the films. They face many challenges when attempting to sell their films in a tough marketplace.

First, most Ugandans don't even know Uganda even makes movies. The first hurdle is to convince a potential buyer to take a chance on something they don't think is possible.

The second hurdle is the cost. A pirated copy of US action movies – *Avengers: End Game* or *John Wick*, for example – can cost as little as 500 UGX. So why would someone pay 2500 UGX for a Ugandan action film?

Movie piracy is rampant in Uganda. Isaac and his team have roughly six days to make money on each new release because that's the time it takes for the bootleggers to copy, label and start selling his film in Kampala for much less than Wakaliwood can afford.

ANCILLARY PRODUCTS

Ever the Filmtrepreneur, Isaac has created a multitude of ancillary products to sell to his worldwide fanbase. He saw a new audience that loved his films and he has created products to serve those customers.

Through his online "SUPA STORE" which can be found on his website wakaliwood.com, he sells hand-painted movie posters on traditional bark cloth, which will run you $200 US, autographed copies of his films on DVD and Blu-Ray, Wakaliwood t-shirts, hats, mugs, stickers, bark cloth magnets, patches, and pins.

REVENUE STREAMS

Isaac has created additional revenue streams for his filmmaking business. He launched a Patreon page where his fans can support his filmmaking by paying a monthly membership to gain access to exclusive Wakaliwood videos and content. As of this writing Isaac generates $840 US per month from his patrons.

I mentioned before that Isaac was uploading videos to YouTube. He has over 100,000 subscribers and generates additional money from advertising revenue from his YouTube channel. A great bonus to running a YouTube channel is you can not only generate revenue from the ads but the videos also promote his upcoming movies and product launches.

PRESS AND MARKETING

Early on, Isaac coined the name "Wakaliwood" to represent the kind of films he makes in the village Wakaliga in Uganda. By creating a brand Isaac's films have traveled the world and has been covered by every major news organization on the planet, from CNN and Vice, to the BBC and Time Magazine. His films have played in film festivals worldwide and even won awards at the genre leading Fantastic Fest Festival.

Isaac is a true Filmtrepreneur, not because he chooses to be but because he needs to be. If his films don't sell his family doesn't eat. He understands his niche audience, saw a hole in the marketplace for Uganda based action films, and filled that hole with his product. He has built a sustainable filmmaking business as an artist in a world that has no high-end filmmaking gear, accessible hard drives, computer gear, IMAX, Netflix, or Apple TV.

He isn't caught up on what the hot new camera is or what editing system he's cutting his latest film on. Isaac just wants to tell stories that mean something to him and his niche audience. Wakaliwood is a perfect example of the regional cinema model.

Isaac and Wakaliwood have taken the Filmtrepreneur spirit and has not only built a sustainable business for himself and his family but he has also created an entire film industry using MiniDV cameras, editing on Adobe Premiere 1.5 and building all his grip equipment, dollies, tripods, camera cranes and movie props from used car parts and lawnmowers. Imagine what you can do. To listen to Isaac's inspiring interview go to www.filmtrepreneur.com/bonus.

CHAPTER 25

How Not to Release a Film

Failures are rarely discussed in case studies but I believe you learn so much more from failing than you do from succeeding. When I set out to produce my extremely ambitious short film *Red Princess Blues* I wanted to not only wow Hollywood with my directing prowess, but being a Filmtrepreneur, I also wanted to show everyone I could have another successful and profitable distribution run of a short film.

Red Princess Blues was supposed to be the short film that skyrocketed my directing career to the stars. Stop me if you heard this one before. The short film would be loved by film festivals all around the world, Hollywood producers would come calling and I'd be directing the feature film version of *Red Princess Blues* by the summer. Unfortunately for me and my bank account it didn't work out exactly the way I planned.

I took the opening five minutes of my feature film screenplay of the same name and expanded it to an 11-minute short film. The budget I had for the film was $50,000, which I was pulling out of savings I had accumulated over the years. Like I said I was going big.

The film's story takes place in a shady carnival underground where carnies drink after work and do ungodly things at a place called the Boneyard. I built huge sets, hired name and Oscar® Nominated actors, collaborated with insanely talented industry professionals, created amazing fight sequences and jaw-dropping visual effects to bring my vision to life.

Me and the star of Red Princess Blues Richard Tyson

When it came to selling this film I didn't want to walk down the same successful and profitable path as I'd done before with my first short film *BROKEN*, my ego just wouldn't allow it. This time I was going to be on the bloody edge of technology and film distribution. The ego is a terrible thing, boys and girls, beware. Sometimes when you aim for the moon you over shoot and land in deep space, cold and alone and that's exactly what happened to me.

In 2010 the world of streaming video was still getting off the ground. Netflix, Amazon and Hulu were just a few years into their streaming offerings but the general public was still watching cable TV. There were no easy ways for independent filmmakers to self-distribute their films to the public.

Then it hit me, I had a revolutionary idea. *Red Princess Blues* will be the first short film to be distributed via downloadable phone app. Brilliant right? I partnered with an app developer and off we went. It took four months to develop the app and cost me $850. Not a bad start-up cost for a new product.

Promotion of the Red Princess Blues App

The app was beautiful, it was essentially a DVD extras package in an app. The app also included a handful of mini-documentaries of the making of the film, a film festival schedule for screenings of the film, exclusive videos, artwork, visual effects breakdowns, behind the scenes photos and links to social media accounts.

I started promoting the film the same way I did *BROKEN*. The problem was that the world had changed in the five years since the release of that short film. The competition in the "online film school / tutorial" space was intense. YouTube had been around for five years already and there were thousands of tutorials already up on the platform. I thought that the unique downloadable app film distribution idea I had come up with would be enough to sell the film, I was terribly wrong.

After the release of the app I sold about 150 copies at $2.99 each, roughly $400 after Apple App Store took their share. For a short film that cost $50,000 and the cost to develop the app was over double my net revenue I was dead in the water. Why did I fail so miserably?

1. I didn't do research to see what products the current marketplace was interested in purchasing
2. I didn't have the money or time to educate the consumer on such a radically new distribution method that no one had ever done before
3. I didn't study the competition
4. I didn't analyze the ROI of the investment in the film or app development
5. I overestimated the need or even desire of the marketplace to watch my film or buy my products

I probably would have been more successful if I had used the *BROKEN* model and just made an intense guerrilla film school on the making of *Red Princess Blues* and sold it on DVD and Blu-Ray. My biggest takeaway was that after my success with making and selling the *BROKEN* DVD my ego was writing checks that my bank account couldn't cash.

I was arrogant enough to believe that if I did it once I could do it again. Just put everything on steroids and your success will be tenfold. Instead of an $8000 budget, let's spend $50,000. Instead of creating a product that the niche audience wants, create a product that is so clever that the customer will be beating your door down to buy it.

So many times Filmtrepreneurs and entrepreneurs create a product that they think or "know" the marketplace wants rather than doing market research and asking to see what the customer might be interested in buying.

Now, it is not all doom and gloom. I did get a few high profile directing gigs based on my work on *Red Princess Blues* that more than paid for the budget of the film, though it did take years for that to happen. The film festival run was extremely successful, which gave me further adventures trying to get the feature film version financed and developed in Hollyweird.

I eventually included the film and mini-documentaries as part of an online course covering how to make and sell short films. That course still generates passive income on a weekly basis.

I took these lessons to heart and this failure shaped how I made and sold indie films moving forward. The budgets of my last two feature films didn't even break $10,000 combined so something must have stuck. To watch the film go to www.filmtrepreneur.com/bonus.

CHAPTER 26

Marketing

Easiest the most important skill a Filmtrepreneur needs to master is marketing. Either they do it themselves or understand the process enough to hire someone to help get the word out on their film projects. Most indie films fail because filmmakers are just not taught the importance of marketing. In the legacy way of doing things the filmmaker would leave the marketing to the distribution company or studio.

That worked years ago when the competition for the consumer's attention was not as intense. In today's world studios, with their multi-million dollar ad campaigns, are having issues reaching the audience. Filmtrepreneurs need to be thinking how they are going to reach their niche audience at the beginning of the development stage. The marketing needs to become part of the creative evolution of the project.

FACEBOOK

Facebook is dead, that is what the headlines are saying. Well, in the world of fake news don't believe everything you see online. Facebook is the eight hundred pound gorilla in the room. With over 2.6 billion users and growing daily, Facebook should not be underestimated.

A few years ago you were able to create a fan page and build an audience fairly easily. If you posted an article or piece of content on your page the majority of your followers would see your content. Then one day Facebook changed the game. You would need to pay or "boost" your content in order to have it seen by your followers. Overnight the social media world changed.

I hear this complaint from filmmakers all the time. You need to pay in order to get your content seen. Yes and no. Filmmaker Jay Shetty has become the most watched filmmaker on Facebook with over 25 million followers. Shetty was able to do this without ever spending a dime to boost or promote his content. His inspirational short films have been viewed over 4 billion times in just a few years. How did he do it?

Shetty understood a very key concept about Facebook's algorithm, that it will expose content that is engaging and that keeps people using the app longer. The more engaging your content, the more eyeballs will see it. Facebook makes more money the longer a user stays on the platform. If your content can do this then Facebook's algorithm will reward you by pumping your content out to more people.

Study what successful Facebook pages and people in your niche are doing. See what kind of content the audience is reacting to. If you are cranking out well-crafted images but your niche audience would really rather consume video content, you will not achieve your goals and blame Facebook for your failure. It takes time to see what works. Market testing is key.

USING FACEBOOK FOR MARKET RESEARCH

One of the greatest research tools available today is Facebook's advertising platform. You can see, almost in real time, how a piece of content will perform within your niche audience.

If you have a trailer for your film and want to see if your audience will respond to it you can test different versions on different segments of your niche. The great part is you can perform these tests with very little money. Usually for $20 or $30 you can get a good idea if your movie trailer is doing what you want it to do.

FACEBOOK ADS

Breaking down Facebook's advertising platform is a deep rabbit hole but I will give you a basic overview. Facebook has created the most powerful marketing machine ever invented in the history of mankind. I know that is a huge claim but it's the truth. Facebook's business model is using its users' information to target their needs and wants with customized advertising and content.

As a marketer you can target your niche audience down to a specific zip code. The power at your finger tips is mind-blowing. If you have a horror film that is a homage to the great 80's slasher films and you want to target that audience, you can pay to show your trailer to people who live in New York, California and Chicago, who like 80's slasher films and are fans of Freddy Krueger, Jason and Chucky, all 80's horror icons.

Then, let's say you happen to have cast a character actor in your film who played a major role in the horror classic *Halloween*. Not only can you target his fans but you can also target fans for the *Halloween* franchise. If you are screening your horror film in your hometown you can target using all the above criteria and limit your ads to only be shown to people who live within a 40 mile radius of the theater.

The possibilities are endless and like I said before you can test your ads or content using these different settings.

GOOGLE ADS

Facebook is not the only player in town. Google is also a very powerful resource. Google Ads allows you to target your audience by two criteria, audience targeting and content targeting. According to Google's website these are the services they provide in each category.

AUDIENCE TARGETING

- Demographics: Target your ads based on how well your products and services trend with users in certain locations, ages, genders, and device types.
- Affinity: Advertisers with TV campaigns can extend a campaign online and reach an audience using Google Search or the Display Network.
- In-market: Show ads to users who have been searching for products and services like yours. These users may be looking to make a purchase, or have previously made a purchase and could still be interested enough to interact with your ads.

- Custom intent: Choose words or phrases related to the people who are most likely to engage with your site and make purchases by using "custom intent audiences." In addition to keywords, custom intent audiences lets you add URLs for websites, apps, or YouTube content related to your audience's interests.
- Similar audiences: Expand your audience by targeting users with interests related to the users in your remarketing lists. These users aren't searching for your products or services directly, but their related interests may lead them to interacting with your ads.
- Remarketing: Target users who have already interacted with your ads, website, or app so that they'll see your ads more often. These users can be in any stage of conversion, as long as they have visited your site or clicked on your ad before. These users may even return to complete a purchase.

CONTENT TARGETING

- Topics: You can target multiple website pages that are relevant to your niche. Topic targeting lets you target a broad range of websites on the Google Ads Display Network.
- Placement: Google allows you to place your ad on websites that would be of interest to your niche audience. You can also target users who visit websites that are in your niche. This is why if you visit a certain site you are followed around by ads for that website no matter where you go online for the next few days.
- Content keywords: You can target keywords relevant to your film or products. Google will target users looking for those key words or phrases. If you want to show your ad in front of anyone who searches for 80's slasher film then this is a great way to target the potential customer.
- Display expansion for search: Google Ads finds customers for you with a combination of smart targeting and automated bidding. This works for both Search and Display campaigns.
  Using Google Ads can be an effective addition to your online marketing strategy.

YOUTUBE ADS

YouTube is part of the Google Ads network but the difference is that you would be using video content in addition to display and banners ads. If you've ever visited YouTube and played a video you will see an ad start to play at the beginning of the video. If you don't want to see it you click on the little button on the bottom right corner that says skip ad after 5 seconds.

You can place your movie trailer or video content in front of people within your audience, by targeting people who consume content related to your niche. YouTube will charge you based on what kind of ad type you choose. If you use TrueView in-stream video ads, you will only pay when a viewer watches your ad for at least 30 seconds or interacts with it by clicking on the link in the video.

YouTube ads generally cost between $0.10 – $0.30 per view, and the views that you generate will count toward your overall YouTube viewer count. For more information on using Facebook, YouTube and Google Ads go to: www.filmtrepreneur.com/bonus.

STOP CALLING IT A WEB SERIES

One of my biggest pet peeves is when filmmakers refer to a series they've produced as a *'Web Series'*. Let me ask you a question, what pops into your head when I tell you I just directed a web series? Probably low production value, no name actors and generally a bad product.

The reason that happens is when filmmakers originally started producing series for the web they were generally horrible. That stigma has stayed with the term "web series." It's all about how you present your product. Branding is key.

I always recommend to my consulting clients with digital series to stop calling it a web series. If you want to automatically add a bit more cache to your project refer to your project as a *'Streaming Series'*.

When I say streaming series what pops into your head? *Stranger Things, House of Cards, Orange is the New Black, The Handmaid's Tale?* Netflix, Hulu and Amazon shows? I think of quality productions, cutting edge content and bigger budgets.

This is just how the mind works. Do yourself a favor and throw your project in the company of the latter. People will give a streaming series more of an opportunity than a web series.

FILMTREPRENEUR POWER MOVE

If you want to take your streaming series or feature film to another level here's a quick hack to that will set you apart. Amazon is the only large streaming platform that grants independent filmmakers the privilege to upload directly to their platform.

This allows you to set a price for rental, purchase and more importantly be a part of Amazon Prime Video. Prime Video is Amazon's subscription streaming service that is part of the extremely popular free shipping Prime membership. This gives you the opportunity to tap into a worldwide audience of millions of people.

You get paid via shared revenue of rentals and purchases. You also get paid a streaming fee per hour for content that is viewed. Once on the platform you can market your streaming series or indie film as an 'Amazon Exclusive' series or film. This adds a tremendous amount of credibility to your project. By doing this, customers will associate your streaming series with all the other streaming series on Amazon.

If you are able to drive traffic to your series you can generate a nice revenue stream. Many filmmakers I know make more money offering their series or feature films on Prime than they do on TVOD rentals and sales. This marketing and branding move can generate more respect, attention and revenue for your web...I mean streaming series.

As a side bonus if you are marketing an Amazon Exclusive Streaming Series sponsors and product placements opportunities might be easier to obtain. Companies are more willing to jump on board an Amazon Exclusive Streaming Series than a web series. The perceived association with Amazon is powerful and something that you should be leveraging.

CHAPTER 27

Film Festivals

Film festivals are a great way to spread the word about your film, receive reviews, and media coverage, not to mention a place to pick up the sought after "Film festival laurel" that you can use to promote your film. Festivals are promotion machines for your film.

With that said, film festivals do not have the ROI that they used to have. In a world of over 5000 film festivals around the planet there are only a few top film festivals that mean anything when it comes to helping you with potential distribution and exposure.

TOP TIER

Depending on your film some of the top tier film festivals like Sundance, Slamdance, SXSW, Cannes, Tribeca, Toronto, and Berlin might be a good fit. Do your research. If you have a bloody horror film, then Sundance might not be a good fit unless you have some major star power in front or behind the camera.

See what films have played at the festival and see if your film would be a good fit. Be honest with yourself because if you aren't, you are just making a donation to the festival by paying the submission fee. Trust me, I've made too many donations to Robert Redford's (the founder of the Sundance Film Festival) retirement account by submitting to his film festival over the years.

MORE IS BETTER

If you submit to all the major film festivals and are not accepted, start submitting to second and third tier film festivals. Try to get accepted to 10-20 film festivals. You can add more if you like. *BROKEN* played in over 180 international film festivals.

Depending on your movie, film festival laurels might be of value marketing to your audience. If you have a drama or thriller laurels add credibility. If you have a comedy or horror film those audiences do not care as much.

HOW TO GET INTO FILM FESTIVAL

I'm not going to beat around the bush, getting into film festivals is tough. There are just too many films being produced today and the competition is fierce. You need to stack the deck in your favor as much as you can. Try to look at the situation from the film festival's point of view. They want to fill theaters. If your film can do that you have a really good chance of getting accepted. I have a few ways to make your film more appetizing to film festivals.

STAR POWER

Just like the studios, film festivals feel much more comfortable programming a film that has movie stars or at least known faces. They are banking that the fans of those movie stars will come out to see their favorite actor at their festivals. This also adds a tremendous amount of credibility to the film festival itself.

By having bigger stars in their lineup, film festivals gain more credibility, not only with potential sponsors and festivalgoers, but with future filmmakers deciding which festival they should submit their films to.

If you were fortunate enough to have visited the Sundance Film Festival in the early days you would understand how much the film lineup landscape has changed. What was once a launching pad for true independent films like *Clerks*, *El Mariachi* and *Puffy Chair* has been replaced with movie star lead "indie films" that were produced for millions of dollars by mini-major studios.

Many filmmakers think that film festivals make the bulk of their revenue from entry fees. This is not the case at all. Yes, it definitely generates income but in many cases that money is used for administrative costs to process the entries themselves. Film festivals live and die with sponsors.

The larger the crowds the better. The more known the stars in the films playing at the festival the better. Festivals need to keep that sponsorship money flowing and movie stars help keep that engine running.

If you can put any star power in your film please do so. If you can cast any known faces from television or Netflix please do so. This will give your film a much better chance of getting programmed. Your personal black and white film made for $10k will have a much tougher time in today's film festival world than it would have had years ago.

I'LL PACK THE HOUSE

Another thing you can do to stack the deck in your favor is to prove to the film festival that you can pack your screenings. Having a large social media presence or audience helps festivals check off that all important box, butts in seats.

Casting an actor, who isn't a household name but does have 3 million Instagram followers will help you and your film stand out of the crowd. Even if the festival shows a bit of interest in your film try to get someone on the phone or email and explain to them your plan for a sellout of your screenings. The larger the social media following is for stars in the film, for the filmmakers and/or for the film itself, the better chance you have for getting programmed.

HAVE A KILLER WEBSITE FOR YOUR FILM

One of the most important elements you need in a marketing plan for an indie film (short, feature or streaming series) today is your website. Imagine going on a date and you want to impress someone but you come dressed in an outfit circa 1996. Probably won't go too well. Not having a website for your film is death but having a poorly designed website is almost worse. Design is so important in every aspect of your writing, producing and marketing of your project.

You can use services like Squarespace.com or Wix.com to create a simple yet elegant website for your film or project. Their platforms have a drag and drop interface and are extremely easy to use.

THE TRAILER

Filmmakers underestimate the power of a great trailer. The trailer for your film will be seen by more people than your full project. A trailer whets the appetite for the film it is promoting, if done well.

Creating movie trailers for action, comedies, sci-fi, and horror films is much easier than other genres. With that said, I've seen some dramas and documentary movie trailers that gave me the chills. It's all about execution. As a storyteller, you have to create an emotional connection with your audience and the trailer is the first line of offense.

If you do not have experience editing movie trailers please don't attempt it. I know you have been editing narrative for a long time but editing movie trailers is an art form all on it's own. My advice is to hire a professional trailer editor who has experience editing trailers in your genre.

THE POSTER

"Give me a poster and a trailer and I can sell any picture." - Slimy Film Distributor.

I would like to think we have evolved beyond the above statement but unfortunately it is still true. Poster artwork is very important in creating a professional and engaging image for your project.

Movie poster from my short film compilation Lipstick and Bullets.
Art by Dan Cregan.

Want to have world class designers battle to give you an amazing movie poster? Then head over to 99Designs.com and check out how they can design your movie poster, business cards, logos, festival fliers and more.

CREATE A LARGER THAN LIFE
IMAGE FOR YOUR PROJECT

When potential film festival programmers come to your website, they will determine in 5 seconds if they are going to watch the trailer. If you create an "event" style website your odds go way up. What I mean is when creating your website you need to create the impression that your film is getting a lot of attention and that it was a well produced and professional project.

When I made my short film *Red Princess Blues*, I had a trailer, press page, wallpaper downloads, behind the scene videos, images, t-shirts, mugs, and I also displayed any festival laurels I had so visitors could see them instantly. This gave my film an edge over the competition as *Red Princess Blues* looked like a big production film and people were talking about it.

The front page of the Red Princess Blues website

Programmers loved it and we played that film in countless film festivals around the world and I only paid for the first 20 festival submissions. Now, the last two tips will bring everything I've been saying together.

EMAIL BABY, IT WORKS!

My films have been in close to 600 film festivals worldwide and I only paid submission fees for a fraction of them. Now all I did was create a few email templates and cold emailed every festival I could get my hands on. I suggest submitting to a ton of festivals for shorts; feature films should be a bit more selective but the above tips still apply.

Having all of the above in place the email I used worked like a charm. I got accepted to maybe 4 out 10 festivals I sent the email to. The basic outline of the email is:

Hello, I'm (insert name) and my film is (insert name).

I was wondering if you were interested in possibly screening (insert name) in this year's festival. If you like the trailer, we would be more than happy to send you a private link to the full length short/feature for your consideration.

Here is a link to the trailer.
Here is a link to the BTS videos of the film.
Here is a quick synopsis.

Thank you again so much for you time.

I also attached the movie poster in the email. This email isn't asking for anything for free. You're just asking to be part of the festival. Now, if the programmer is interested, then they'll email you back explaining to you how to submit. At this point you send them a follow up email.

Here is what I wrote:

Thanks for getting back to us. I hate to ask (and to be honest embarrassed to ask) but we are respectfully requesting a waiver of the entry fee to submit to your festival. We have already exhausted our entire film & promotion budget and would still love to be a part of your festival. We put everything we had up on the screen =)

Please let us know. If you like the trailer, we would be more than happy to send you a private link to the full short/feature for your consideration. Thank you again so much for you time.

After this I would get into 40%-60% of the festivals I sent this email to. Now if they email you back and say "no" you have one more chance. If I wanted to get into the festival that bad I would say:

I completely understand. I have an idea, if you like, we can send you a copy of (insert film name), if you like it and accept it into the festival we would be more than happy to pay the entry fee. It's just so expensive to shell out cash for festivals and not get shown. What do you think? Thanks so much for your understanding and consideration.

I'm not about screwing over film festivals out of entry fees but I just want things to be fair. Spending $25-$50 on an entry fee and have no guarantee of play in the festival is nuts to me. If you have to pay $25 to get screened at a festival I'm cool with that.

Many festivals just want great content on the screen and in many cases they'll let you in for free. The thousands of film festivals worldwide are all looking for amazing content to fill their lineups.

DO YOUR FESTIVAL RESEARCH

Not every film festival is right for every indie film. Just as you have niched down to your target audience you should also niche down to the film festivals you are submitting to. If you have a horror film, then go after the top tier horror and fantasy film festivals.

If you have certain themes in your film like LGBT, cultural, ethnic, spiritual, or sports, for example, target film festivals that focus on those niches. You'll have a much better chance of getting accepted and winning some awards. For a deeper dive into film festivals, editing movie trailers and poster design ideas go to www.filmtrepreneur.com/bonus.

A WORD ON SUNDANCE

The Sundance Film Festival is the gold standard for film festivals in the United States and around the world. Every filmmaker I know has at one time or another submitted a film to the festival in hopes of getting that magical call from the programmer saying you've been accepted.

We are all looking for that lottery ticket, that same ticket that Kevin Smith, Steven Soderbergh, Edward Burns, Robert Rodriguez and Mark and Jay Duplass got. The raw truth is that for most indie films that call will never come. In 2018, Sundance received 14,200 submissions and less than a couple of hundred feature and short films received that magical phone call.

You have to understand that film festivals are not the only way to get your films out there anymore. Sure, getting into Sundance would be AMAZING but for the majority it isn't meant to be and, you know what?…that's OK.

This shouldn't stop you from moving forward on your filmmaking journey. Film festivals are run by people with tastes and opinions. Those tastes might not be in line with your tastes and that's OK. Maybe you made an amazing film but there were three other films about the same subject so they had to flip a coin.

Getting into Sundance is a lottery ticket for sure but it isn't as important as it used to be. Here's what filmmaker and Sundance Alumni Mark Duplass tweeted about it:

"Annual Sundance Film Festival rejection reminder: Sundance is awesome, but Sundance is not everything. So many incredible films don't make the cut. Don't let it get you down. If you believe in your film, keep pushing forward. There are so many new ways to get it there. Good luck!"
– *Mark Duplass*

I couldn't have said it better myself. Film festivals are just one of many ways you can get attention for your film. Keep that in mind the next time you get a festival rejection email in your inbox.

CHAPTER 28

Test, Adjust, and Pivot

As Filmtrepreneurs you need to be able to try new approaches and test those ideas again and again to see what works. This goes for not only your marketing but also with your product lines, film production techniques, distribution models, financing and every other facet of the Filmtrepreneur Method.

You may have heard of the 10,000 hours rule popularized by author Malcom Gladwell. He proposed that anyone can become a master of anything if they practice for 10,000 hours. But there's another thesis that might be even more powerful, the 10,000 experiment rule.

Empact founder Michael Simmons proposes that you follow the lead of giants like Facebook, Netflix, Amazon and even Leonardo Da Vinci. The rule simply states "deliberate experimentation is more important than deliberate practice in a rapidly changing world."

Thomas Edison tested 967 ways to make a light bulb work before he had his eureka moment. It was his relentless nature that finally brought him success. The more experiments you do the odds fall much more in your favor.

According to one of Leonardo Da Vinci's biographers, Walter Isaacson, Da Vinci would create a "to-test" list rather than a "to-do" list. Isaacson states "Every morning his life hack was: make a list of what he wants to know. Why do people yawn? What does the tongue of a woodpecker look like?" Da Vinci's love for experimenting proved to be a cornerstone of his legendary success in art, science, human anatomy and engineering.

Facebook founder Mark Zuckerberg stated in an interview "One of the things I'm most proud of and that is really the key to our success is this testing framework ... At any given point in time, there isn't just one version of Facebook running. There are probably 10,000."

Experiment with your movie trailers, your poster designs and see what works and what doesn't. Use Facebook to market test your ideas, from pre-production to product ideas inspired by the final film. Facebook has amazing analytics that you should be taking full advantage of.

You can see in real-time what is working and what is not. Don't be afraid to fail. Failing is what will make you succeed. All filmmaking careers are forged in the fire of failure. Remember this as you walk your filmmaking path.

DON'T GET EMOTIONAL

Now that you are testing every element of your project, you will start getting an amazing amount of data. A trap you might fall into is not listening to the data, no matter how painful it might be. You might have put an immense amount of time and energy into a product, film project or movie trailer and as you begin the experimenting process, the marketplace is not responding as you had hoped.

You will be tempted to rationalize to yourself why the data is wrong to lessen the blow to your ego. I know I did, as I detailed earlier in my story of the failed *Red Princess Blues* App idea that went south. I talked myself into believing everything would be all right as long as I kept going. I put good money after bad and lost. The filmmaking ego is a powerful foe you need to be aware of.

When the data is not to their liking filmmakers will talk themselves and their team into believing that everything is fine and it will all work out. A Filmtrepreneur will analyze the data and make a pivot if needed without emotion. It is imperative to become fluid with your thinking and make any adjustments you need based on the data you are getting from the marketplace. If you can't make that call then find someone who can, if not you can sink your entire film project before it ever has a chance to launch.

BLOCKBUSTER VIDEO: A CAUTIONARY TALE

In the late 80's and through the early 2000's *Blockbuster Video* rose to power as the video store to beat. They dominated the space with over 9094 rental store locations worldwide at its peak in 2004. The bigger they are the harder they fall. Blockbuster's management had focused on their core product, which was renting and selling used VHS and then DVDs. They couldn't fathom any other way of doing business. They had been so successful doing things the same way why would they change a winning formula?

Then came a little start-up called *Netflix*. They had a revolutionary idea of renting DVDs through the mail via a subscription model and doing away with the dreaded late fees. If you rented a film at a video store and returned it late, the store would charge a late fee. This was a major pain point for the consumer.

By doing away with late fees and giving customers access to rent as many films as they could a month, based on their subscription plan, Netflix grew incredibly fast. By the time the dinosaurs over at Blockbuster started to take notice, Netflix had taken a huge bite out of the marketplace once dominated solely by them.

Blockbuster started their own mail order rental service to challenge Netflix but they struggled to compete. Over at Netflix everything was not as rosy as it seemed. In 2000 Netflix founder Reed Hastings approached Blockbuster's top brass with a potential buyout proposition. Hastings asked for $50 million to give away his company. The evil ego rose its ugly head and Blockbuster, thinking Netflix was a small niche company, declined the offer.

As we all know Netflix later introduced the concept of streaming movies via the Internet and single-handedly disrupted the entire film industry. At the last evaluation Netflix was worth over $120 billion. Blockbuster's inability to see the writing on the wall and pivot was its downfall. The company shuttered its doors in 2013 and became a cautionary tale of what happens when you are too rigid with your thinking.

We live in an ever changing world. What might have been true last year is no longer true today. The marketplace is shifting faster than we can keep up. How different are the viewing habits of today's world versus just ten years ago? If you do not have a fluid mindset and are willing to constantly experiment and try new ways of doing things you will be left behind. Don't become Blockbuster.

CHAPTER 29

Expand and Grow

Now that your film is generating revenue it's time to think about how you can further be of service to the audience you have cultivated. To this point in the process we have created multiple revenue streams from your feature film.

During this time you'll expand and build a larger foundation that you will be able to launch future film projects from. Let's use my vegan chef romantic comedy, *Crazy Sexy Vegan* as an example to give you a few ideas that will help you expand and grow your Filmtrepreneurial business.

SUBSCRIPTION SERVICE / MEMBERSHIP SITE

Crazy Sexy Vegan is off and running. You have multiple revenue streams coming in from online courses, cookbooks, apparel sales, On-Demand screenings in cities around the country, international sales, and SVOD, AVOD and TVOD revenue from your film. Now let's expand and grow the business.

You see the online education you created is doing well so you put out a feeler and ask your audience if they would be interested in a potential streaming service or online membership. This service would give them exclusive access to all your online education content plus new content that will help them on their vegan journey.

Based on their response you can create a membership site through a platform like Teachable.com or create a full-blown streaming service accessible on Apple TV, iPhone, Android, Roku and Amazon. If that is the way you want to go you can use a company like Uscreen.tv, a platform that allows you to create a full-blown streaming service at a very affordable price.

Creating a monthly revenue stream using a membership site is how Netflix became a multibillion-dollar company. Amazon's Prime membership generates over $12 billion a year for the online giant.

Building out a membership site doesn't have to be a huge undertaking. I've seen membership sites that are big on exclusive information and training and very light on high-end production value. You'll have to cater the product to the audience you are selling to. Some audiences want the bells and whistles and others just want access to information. Either way it is a massive way you can grow your revenue exponentially.

BOOK OF THE MONTH CLUB

Developing a Book of the Month club for your audience is a great way to be of more service to a hungry customer base. If you have built a strong connection with your niche, then offering them monthly or quarterly books on a subject matter they are already interested in is a no brainer.

Depending on your niche you could reach out to publishers and purchase titles in bulk to ship out. You'd be surprised at how receptive publishers would be to this proposition. They are supportive of anything that sells more books.

This would be a monthly subscription where you could offer the book of the month or, if quarterly, 2-3 books. In addition you can include a custom synopsis of each book, video breakdowns of the book, ebook, an audiobook version, and maybe even access to exclusive author interviews. It's all up to you and what makes sense for your niche.

WORKSHOPS/SEMINARS

Another often overlooked possible revenue stream is workshops. Depending on your niche you could generate a massive revenue stream from live workshops and seminars.

If I use *Crazy Sexy Vegan* as an example I could create cooking demonstrations, speak about how to transition to a more plant-based diet, include meditation classes and guest speakers. If you have a horror niche you can focus on the making and selling horror films and maybe do a special effect makeup seminar if you have cultivated horror filmmakers in your community. Another bonus is that you can sell other products and services to your workshop audience generating even more revenue.

Recording the workshop and selling it as a stand-alone online video course or as part of a membership site are other potential revenue streams. You could even release it as an audiobook, which you can sell yourself or through Audible.com. You just have to be creative and see if your audience would find value in any of these ideas.

SPEAKING

If you establish yourself as a thought leader in your space you could easily charge for speaking engagements. Just by being a director or producer of a popular niche film you automatically have credibility in the space. Many filmmakers I know have been able to make a nice side income by speaking at schools, events, film festivals, and conventions.

– CASE STUDY –

Food Matters

A perfect example of Filmtrepreneurs expanding and growing their business based off of one or more films is the case of *Food Matters*, a documentary about nutrition.

Filmmakers James Colquhoun and Carlo Ledesma directed this game-changing documentary and in the film they present a thesis that diet plays a huge part in treating a wide range of illnesses and health conditions such as diabetes, heart disease, depression, and cancer. From that one film independently produced, James and his wife Laurentine ten Bosch have built an empire.

With their first film they were able to cultivate a niche audience that were interested in weight loss, curing health conditions, general healthy eating, plant-based diets, meditation, exercise and yoga.

They further grew that audience with their other films *Hunger for Change* and the docu-series *Transcendence*. Being true Filmtrepreneurs, as they grew their tribe they began to create other ways to be of service to them. The list of products and services they developed is pretty remarkable.

- DVD and Blu-Rays of their films
- A library of Food Matters Print Books
- Detox Guides
- Recipe eBooks
- Food Matters Mason Jars
- Food Matters Gratitude Bracelets
- Food Matters Inspirational Magnets
- Food Matters Organic Towels
- Food Matters Super Greens Supplement
- Food Matters Tote Bags
- Essential Oils
- One-on-One Coaching
- Wellness Retreats
- Directory of Health Care Coaches / Consultants
- FMTV Streaming Service

That last one is the most impressive revenue stream of the bunch for me. *Food Matters TV* is a one stop shop for documentaries and series about all the core interests of their audience, plant-based diets, stress management, meditation, inspirational stories and yoga to name a few. With FMTV they were able to tap into a need that their audience wanted filled.

On their streaming service they were able to build a library of not just their own content but of other filmmakers' films as well, which turned them into a Netflix of health and wellness. The brilliant part of this business model is that every time someone watches either of their films, Food Matters or Hunger for Change, out in the world they are introduced to their online eco-system.

Both *Food Matters* and *Hunger for Change* are available on all major streaming platforms, so they are able to tap into those massive audiences as well. The films are acting as a marketing machine that doesn't sleep.

When that interested customer finds their website they have the products and services that the person is searching for. Since they already have created a bond with the *Food Matters* brand, sales become much easier.

James and Laurentine are a remarkable example of what filmmakers can do with a film if they think like Filmtrepreneurs.

RINSE AND REPEAT

The purpose of the Filmtrepreneur Method is not only to create one profitable project but to build on each success to create a portfolio of films that continuously generate revenue for you. I've been able to build a portfolio of short and feature films that brings in passive income each month. I leveraged those projects and also created multiple ancillary products, services and companies I use to better serve the communities I've cultivated.

So many filmmakers put everything they have into the one project in hopes that that film will launch their careers or that they will make a bundle of cash from it. Filmtrepreneurs can't think this way. They can't only think of the one project, they need to think more long-term.

Focus on one project at a time but always keep the long game in the back of your mind. The more projects, products and services you have in your portfolio the more income you will generate and the better you will be able to serve your niche audience.

SERVING MULTIPLE NICHES

There are two ways you can build up your portfolio. You can focus on one niche, cultivate that niche and continue to create films, products and services for that niche. Living in that world for many projects to come. That is a great way to apply the Filmtrepreneur Method.

If you are a sci-fi filmmaker and love making science fiction genre films then more power to you. The wonderful part of this method is that you can leverage the existing niche with each new project. You will also build a reputation within that niche which makes it much easier to see ancillary products and services from each project.

But if you don't want to live in the science fiction space forever and want to venture out into other niches you can do that as well. There are two sides to this method. It will be a bit more time-consuming jumping into a new niche because you will need to repeat the entire process of cultivating the new audience you want to create a film for. You will also not be able to leverage your existing audience.

On the other hand, diversifying your portfolio by creating different projects in different niches could also be extremely beneficial. If the science fiction indie film niche becomes too competitive and it's harder to get attention in that space, then you are in a bad place.

But if you have cultivated another audience in the extreme sports niche then you can lean on that audience instead. Creating multiple niche audiences is much more time-consuming but it will make your portfolio more resilient to the marketplace. If your creative spirit wants to stay in one place that's fine; just understand the potential long-term risks.

You could also venture out into another sub-niche within your main niche. Using horror again, if your first project was an 80's slasher film you could make your next film a ghost story. This way you can leverage your existing audience, cultivate the new sub-niche and spread your creative wings.

The marketplace for feature films is changing so rapidly that the industry itself has no idea what's coming around the corner. Always think about your films, products and services in the long-term.

CHAPTER 30

Reversing the Filmtrepreneur Method

Why would you want to reverse the Filmtrepreneur Method? Let me explain. This entire book has been focused on turning your feature film, series or video content into a business. What if you already have a business and want to use a feature film, series or video content to drive revenue to it or even expand an existing brand?

Many in my community know that I used to own an olive oil gourmet company in Los Angeles. Don't ask why, that is a story for another book. When I ran that company I used video to brand, build, and drive sales. I launched two weekly streaming series focusing on olive oil, aged balsamic vinegar and drink mixology.

Every week I would release an episode answering a question about EVOO (extra virgin olive oil) or 18-year-aged balsamic vinegar. These were free series that provided value to anyone who was interested in those topics.

I hosted the series on YouTube and Vimeo, as well as on my own website. By being of service to my customers I gained their loyalty and established myself as an authority in the space. This created huge benefits for my company.

- Increased sales
- Drove new attention to my company's brand

- Established me as an authority within the niche
- Added credibility for any new customers who came to my website
- New customers recognized my company at events we sold at

The cost to create the streaming series was minimal and the ROI and ROT was exponential. The first series did so well that I launched a second series focusing on an underserved niche within my customer base, mixologists. Yes, mixologists.

I was noticing that a few forward-thinking bartenders were purchasing my 18-year-aged flavored balsamic vinegars by the case for their bars and using them to create original cocktails for their customers. I saw an opportunity.

I hired an actor, and we were off. After launching the second series my sales of balsamic vinegar went up. Again the ROI and ROT was well worth the time and money I invested.

– CASE STUDY –

Wine Library TV

Author, blogger and serial entrepreneur Gary Vaynerchuk's story is the definition of the reverse Filmtrepreneur Method. Gary created a successful lemonade franchise at the age of 7, sold tens of thousands of dollars in baseball cards while in high school and at the age of 14 he joined the family business which was his father's liquor store.

Gary saw the potential of this thing called "the Internet" and slowly convinced his father to change the name of his store from "Shoppers Discount Liquors" to one of the first online, e-commerce platforms called Wine Library.

Gary then launched one of the first episodic video shows on YouTube in 2006 called Wine Library TV. He realized that there was an underserved audience within his niche of wine lovers, the everyman, and decided to be of service to that community.

His show focused on wine from an everyman's point of view by taking away the pretentiousness that had been associated with being a wine connoisseur. Some of his shows would cover which wines pair well with a Big Mac or does a red wine pair well with Captain Crunch cereal.

Being so forward-thinking, Wine Library TV was the first show of its kind online for the wine industry. He produced that show every day for over 5 years, almost never missing an episode.

With Gary's help, the revenue of his father's business exploded from $3 million a year to over $60 million. Gary went on to be a thought leader in his space and wrote multiple best sellers. I recommend his seminal books *Crush It!: Why NOW Is the Time to Cash In on Your Passion* and *The Thank You Economy* to anyone interested in selling a product to a customer in today's world.

PRODUCT PLACEMENT IN REVERSE

When I made my film *On the Corner of Ego and Desire* I looked around at the resources I had and backed into the writing of the scriptment. One of the resources I had to use was my *Indie Film Hustle Podcast*.

I wrote the film about filmmakers trying to track down a big time film producer, why not have them make a stop at the *Indie Film Hustle Podcast* on their journey. The product was perfectly aligned with the needs of the story and with my niche audience.

I even made a cameo as myself furthering the branding of *Indie Film Hustle* in the film. Trust me, if I could have had an actor play me I would have but, unfortunately, I had to make an appearance.

If you are an indie filmmaker watching a movie about filmmakers trying to sell their film at the Sundance Film Festival do you think that audience might be interested in listening to a free filmmaking resource like the *Indie Film Hustle Podcast*? I think they would.

Just so that you are aware I'm using this method right now as you are reading this book. I'm using my film and podcast as case studies. Will you search out my film to watch it, I don't know, but chances are you might. Here, let me make it easy for you; just go to www.egoanddesirefilm.com for my film and www.filmmakingpodcast.com to subscribe to the *Indie Film Hustle Podcast*. As they say don't hate the player hate the game.

All hustling aside, I'm using this as an example to show you how powerful it is to place a product in a film, in this case my IFH Podcast, with an audience that it is aligned with it. I'm not creating my film or the podcast for this book, those products already exist. I'm using this product, the book, to drive traffic and attention to my existing products and further be of service to my audience.

The brilliant thing about reversing the Filmtrepreneur Method is that you already have a business, product lines, marketing, and delivery infrastructures in place. You are using video content to drive sales.

– CASE STUDY –

The Barn Theatre - Tomorrow's Stars Today

Filmmaker Phillip Wurtzel was thinking like a reverse Filmtrepreneur when he produced the film *The Barn Theatre: Tomorrow's Stars Today*. In 1946, Jack and Betty Ragotzy opened The Barn Theatre in a small town in South West Michigan.

For over seven decades The Barn has trained some of the biggest names on Broadway and Hollywood through their summer stock acting program. Some of the names that went through The Barn's doors are Diane Ladd, Dana Delany, Jennifer Garner, Tom Wopat, Laura Graham, and Adrienne Barbeau to name a few.

Wurtzel saw an opportunity and approached the owners and proposed producing a documentary chronicling the history of The Barn Theater. They agreed and Wurtzel was off and running. He was also able to create multiple revenue streams from the film including international sales and domestic TVOD, SVOD and AVOD revenue. He also was able to negotiate the one very important thing, he carved out DVD rights for the film.

Wurtzel partnered with the owners of the theater and they agreed to place the DVD of the film in the theater gift shop. Hundreds if not thousands of guests pass through the doors every season and what better souvenir to buy than a DVD. The film was also a win for the owners of the Theater. The documentary acts as a huge advertisement for the theater and the acting school they run.

The niche audience that's watching this film more than likely have a few actors in it and they might apply to the summer stock acting program. The film will be a lead generator for not only fresh actors looking for a top-notch acting program but for theatergoers who might be interested in seeing what The Barn Theater has to offer each season.

Wurtzel knew that there was a niche audience of patrons that would be interested in a documentary covering the rich history of the theater.

He kept his budget low, had the theater as an outlet to sell his film, and created a passive revenue stream that he'll be collecting for years to come.

If you are looking for a topic, idea or story for your feature film or documentary why not approach an existing business and see if you can help each other out. Tapping into an existing business' audience and product line might be a perfect fit for your film project. Filmtrepreneurs are always looking for any advantage that can help them in the marketplace.

This is very powerful stuff and should be in the toolbox of any Filmtrepreneur. If you want to partner with a business, have an existing business or product and you want to drive revenue think about using the Reverse Filmtrepreneur Method.

CHAPTER 31

Side Hustles the Filmtrepreneur

When you start down your Filmtrepreneur path you will need to create immediate revenue streams that do not rely completely on a niche audience or specific film projects. This is where the side hustle comes in. For as long as I could remember I always had side hustles going on. From putting up weekly garage sales at ten years old to selling baseball cards to buying used video games and DVDs and selling them on Amazon.

The side hustles were what kept food on the table when my freelance work was slow. Side hustles need to be in every Filmtrepreneur's toolbox. Think of side hustles as revenue streams, the more hustles, the more money comes into your bank account. I could write an entire book on side hustles for filmmakers and screenwriters but until I do here are a few key side hustles that will keep the money flowing while you build your Filmtrepreneur empire.

HOURS FOR DOLLARS

I got my start as a freelance editor. I worked on music videos, commercials, corporate, TV promos, documentaries and films. This was how I made the bulk of my income when I began my filmmaking journey. Even if you have a full-time job that just pays the bills you can always freelance on the side.

Ask yourself what skill set do you have that you could charge money for? I always suggest you look for a freelance side hustle within the film industry. There you will build relationships and make contacts that could help you on your path. You could also freelance in other areas that could be beneficial to your Filmtrepreneurial projects, like online marketing, graphic design, t-shirt manufacturer, or film schools just to name a few.

When creating this freelance side hustle don't focus just on the money you could earn but how it can help you in the long term. What skills will I learn doing this? Who will I potentially meet? The Filmtrepreneur always thinks about the long game and not just the short-term.

STOCK FOOTAGE

The online stock footage industry has exploded in the past ten years. The Internet has allowed anyone with a camera and some talent to upload their footage and make money. If you own or can borrow a professional camera you can get into the stock footage game. Whether you are using old footage sitting on your hard drive or going out to create new footage specifically for stock, you can begin to generate a nice revenue stream. Some of the biggest stock footage websites are:

- Shutterstock
- iStockPhoto
- Pond5
- Getty Images
- Fotosearch
- Videohive
- Storyblocks Video

The problem with uploading stock footage is dealing with all of different stock footage companies. Having to set up accounts on each website and manually upload, meta tag, write a description and add keywords is a pain. To solve this irritating barrier of entry I use a Black-Box. Blackbox is a free platform that allows the video creator to upload any stock footage once and have it submitted to all the major stock footage websites.

Then Blackbox handles all the business. When you get a sale it comes into your account and money is sent monthly to your PayPal account.

As an experiment I uploaded a handful of clips from some old projects to see what would happen. To my surprise I made multiple sales.

What I love about this side hustle is that it's a passive source of income. Once you upload everything you don't need to do any other work. The more clips you put up, the more potential for income you will have. For more resources on stock footage as a side hustle go to www. filmtrepreneur.com/bonus.

STOCK MOTION GRAPHICS

If you have the skills, creating stock motion graphics is a great side hustle. Filmmakers and content creators are always looking for graphic packages that can save them time and money. Some of the most popular kind of stock motion graphics are:

- Lower Thirds Animations
- Logo Design
- Opening Credits
- Production Company Logo Opens
- Main Titles
- End Credit Crawls
- Background animations

You can either just sell pre-built animations with no customizations like lower thirds and background animations or created custom motion graphics ala carte, which makes this a bit more freelance. Another way would be to provide the customer with the full Adobe After Effects, or whatever software you are using, project file with all the elements included so they can customize the graphics to their needs.

It doesn't just stop at motion graphics, an entire industry has developed around this side hustle. Now the opportunities are endless. Here are a few other products you could offer.

- After Effects Presets
- After Effects Templates
- DaVinci Resolve Macros
- DaVinci Resolve Templates

- Final Cut Pro Templates
- Premiere Rush Templates
- Premiere Pro Presets
- Premiere Pro Templates

Many of the same websites that allow you to upload stock footage will also accept motion graphics. Here are a few other websites that accept stock motion graphics or allow you to sell your motion graphic skills as a freelancer.

- Fivver.com
- Upwork.com
- Videohive.net

Just like shooting stock footage, once you upload your motion graphics or the project files, you don't need to do any more work for this passive income stream or you can turn this into a freelance side hustle; it's completely up to you.

RENT YOUR FILM GEAR

A new side hustle that has popped up in recent years is the filmmaker-to-filmmaker gear rental business. If you own any film gear like cameras, lenses, lights, or drones you can rent them out for a side income when you are not using them.

One of the platforms I recommend in the space is Sharegrid.com. You go to the website, list your gear and wait for the rentals to come in. Don't worry about insurance, they have that covered as well so your gear is safe. I know filmmakers making a very nice side income renting their gear. This will help you pay off the new camera so you can be in full profit faster.

Also, if you are a filmmaker looking for film gear at a reasonable rate for one of your productions you can rent gear here as well. Another bonus is you are talking to another filmmaker, not necessarily a rental house. This is a great way to network with other filmmakers who you could possibly collaborate with in the future.

At the moment these kinds of companies are mainly in big cities but they are expanding to more and more locations every month.

AFFILIATE MARKETING

Another way you could generate revenue from an existing niche audience is by affiliating marketing. Affiliating Marketing is when you recommend a product or service to an audience and you earn a commission if they decide to purchase the item or service.

Let me give you an example. Amazon.com has one of the world's largest and most successful affiliate marketing programs. Amazon has over 900,000 affiliates in its program and about 23% of all the traffic that comes into Amazon is from referrals.

If I have a website or Facebook page focusing on *Star Wars* fandom I could sign up for the Amazon affiliate program and start promoting *Star Wars* products to my audience. I just grab a referral link to the product I want to recommend, write an article and place the Amazon link to the product in the post.

When someone comes to read my *Star Wars* article and they click on the link it takes them to the *Star Wars* product on Amazon. If they buy that specific product or anything else on the site within 24 hours you earn a percentage of the sale. The commission amounts vary from product category but you get the idea.

You can also use this same technique with YouTube videos, your own personal website or any social media account; basically anywhere you can place a link you can make a side income from affiliate marketing.

If you read a book and want to recommend it to your friends grab an affiliate link from Amazon and make a commission. There's no additional cost to the buyer so you are providing a valuable service to the customer by recommending products they might like.

There are hundreds of companies that run affiliate programs with thousands of companies, products and services you can promote. Here are a few of the big ones.

- Amazon Associates
- eBay Partner Network
- ShareASale.com
- ClickBank
- CJ Affiliate
- PartnerStack

• Fiverr Affiliates Program

A warning, if you only chase the almighty dollar with affiliate marketing you will not do well. People will see through you and you will waste a ton of time. You need to focus on being of service to the audience you are recommending products and services to. The more authentic you can be in any kind of marketing the better.

All it takes for this side hustle is your time and energy. There are people who are full-time affiliate marketers and make hundreds of thousands of dollars a month. So whether a side hustle or full time gig you can make a nice income from affiliate marketing.

CREATE A COURSE

You could create an online course on a subject you have some expertise in. Your course doesn't have to be specifically about filmmaking. You can focus on online marketing, computers, editing, meditation, working out, football coaching or pretty much anything you can think of.

Once you create an online course you can uploaded it to platforms like Udemy.com or Skillshare.com. You can set this up as a purely passive income and not put any more time or energy into it or you can put a small amount of effort marketing the courses to get a bigger return.

Many filmmakers I know have focused 100% of their energies in creating online education for these platforms and many generate tens of thousands of dollars a month. Online education is not going anywhere. You can tap into this industry for little or no money and generate a nice side or full income depending on your goals.

SELL SHORT FILM SCRIPTS

I had never heard of this side hustle until I met a 17-year-old writer/director by the name of Jonathan Perry. When I had the pleasure of interviewing this young man he revealed to me that he was able to generate over $10,000 selling short film scripts to the highest bidder. He was basically a ghost screenwriting mercenary. He would not only sell his scripts, he would sell the copyright to them as well and take no credit. How did he do this?

By searching for screenwriting blogs that had public message boards and posting on those forums. He would create a paragraph pitch and add a link to the script. Once posted he would take feedback and offers. Jonathan had some advice for any ghost screenwriters out there.

"Don't expect to sell to just people on the blogs, build a connection with active members and maybe they will know someone who might be interested. It can take a couple of weeks to state your intentions and work on a busy blog. Don't stress if you don't find a marketplace right away, but have scripts ready. Just get it written, so write, write, write!"

Jonathan thought outside the box and created a nice side hustle for himself. If you are willing to be a ghostwriter of short films for other filmmakers, then this could be a great side hustle for you. If you want to hear more on Jonathan's method and story go to www.filmtrepreneur. com/bonus.

CHAPTER 32

Art vs. Commerce

Now that we have taken the journey of the Filmtrepreneur together I wanted to address something that is too often brought up, the battle of art vs. commerce. Many filmmakers believe that filmmaking is an art form, as do I. Filmmaking is a beautiful, powerful and emotional art form. It is unique because filmmaking brings together many other art forms and disciplines to bring it alive.

Unfortunately, filmmaking is also one of the most expensive art forms ever created. The cost of our paint, brushes and canvas can be astronomical. If you plan to be a filmmaker who makes more than one film in his or her life then you better come to grips that this art form is also a business.

Most filmmakers don't have the luxury of experimenting with millions of dollars of other people's money. Our canvas is extremely expensive. We also can't create the art without a team of people. It's an art form that demands collaboration. This all costs money.

So many times I wish I could just pick up a guitar and express myself as an artist but alas I worked in a video store in high school and the film-making bug infected me there. There is no immunization from that bug; once you are bitten, it's with you for life.

With all that said, do you need to make loads of money on every feature film you create? Absolutely not. If you have a story that is burning in your heart to tell and it might only be interesting to ten people in the world then by all means make that film.

The only thing you need to understand is that you will have to make that film on a budget that you are willing to lose. Keep your budget low enough that you can take the financial hit but high enough so you can realize your vision.

When I directed my film *On the Corner of Ego and Desire*, making money was not on my mind. It was an experimental film for sure. It was a story I wanted to tell and since I made it for a budget of around $3000 I could take the chance of shooting a feature film during the Sundance Film Festival, with actors I'd never met, with a scriptment, and in four days. I did apply the Filmtrepreneur Method to the making of that film but money was not the driving force for shooting that project.

The Filmtrepreneur Method is there to help you on your filmmaking path. Why can't you do both, make the movie you want to produce and also think about the business side as well?

CHAPTER 33

This is Just the Beginning

When I sat down to write this book my goal was to change the way filmmakers thought about how a movie needs to be produced, marketed and sold to the public. I wanted filmmakers to understand that there is another way; that you don't need to give your film away to a middleman or some predatory distribution company in hopes that one day they might send you a check in the mail.

The legacy filmmaking paradigm taught around the world is out of date for today's ever changing marketplace. What is true today will most definitely change in the next six months.

When the music industry was under attack by piracy via digital downloads they didn't embrace the new technology or even try to understand what was going on, they just went on the defensive. The dinosaurs that ran the record labels were more interested in keeping the status quo in place.

Because of their inability to change and adjust to the marketplace, and its customers' needs, the entire industry came crumbling down. To this day the legacy record labels that survived are still having problems adapting to the new-world of music.

Even recording artists had to adjust. Record sales and publishing rights no longer generated the revenue of yesteryear. Artists needed to adapt. The ones who did, survived and thrived. The ones who just sat there complaining about how things were changing didn't.

Artists had to start thinking like entrepreneurs. The smart ones built entire businesses around their brand, music and image. They created ancillary products for their fans to purchase. They went on tour more often to sell not only tickets but their products as well. They used the record labels for distribution and marketing. Artists were no longer owned by the record labels, the smart ones partnered with them. They became the CEO of their careers and made a business out of their art.

I don't want independent filmmakers to fall victim to the same mistakes that destroyed Blockbuster Video or brought down the legacy music industry. If you think it's hard to make money with your films now using this out of date distribution model, just wait, it will get even harder moving forward.

If you stay on the path that has been laid out in front of you by the powers that be, you will not be ready to thrive in the new-world of independent filmmaking, video content and how it is consumed.

Don't be afraid of change; embrace it. Methods of film distribution will change. New, cheaper cinema cameras and lenses will be developed. New business models, online platforms, and opportunities will be invented. But being of service to a community you are trying to sell to will never change. I hope this book makes you think differently about your chosen art form.

I want the Filmtrepreneur Method to empower you as an independent filmmaker to be able to make as many feature films, streaming series and any other content as you wish. Remember "There is the word show and the word business and the word business has twice as many letters as the word show."

When you have the BUSINESS side covered then you can make as much SHOW as you like. I found the business side of making films as creative as the making of the films themselves. Figuring out revenue streams, ancillary product lines, marketing strategies and distribution is part of the creative process in my world.

Go out there and take risks, fail and fail often so you may learn what not to do and add more experience to your Filmtrepreneur toolbox. Make films, educate yourself as much as you can every day and keep on hustling toward your dream.

Take each day, step-by-step, inch-by-inch. You can walk anywhere as long as you keep taking one small step at a time. The power to change your life is in your hands, not in some God from Mount Hollywood. Don't ever forget that.

Filmmaking is your dream and it's your responsibility to make it happen; if not, why else are we here? Be of service to as many people as you can with your films, work, and products. As the saying goes "If you want your dreams to come true, help someone else with theirs."

Good luck to you on your Filmtrepreneurial journey and as always keep that hustle going, keep that dream alive and I'll see you at the movies and the bank.

EPILOGUE

Careful What You Wish For

Many filmmakers want to cut the line or hack the system to get to their dreams that much faster. I understand this completely because I had that mindset for most of my career. But if you get to the top of the mountain by a hack you will not have the skills and experience needed to navigate the tough terrain.

This is why, within five years of winning a jackpot, 80% of lottery winners end up in a worse financial situation than they were before they were handed that big check. They don't value the wealth because they did nothing to earn it. They never had to struggle to get it and don't have the tools or mindset to handle that amount of money.

I know it's hard climbing your own personal mountain. You will stumble, fall and fail again and again. That experience is what gives you the tools needed to navigate the tough terrain. Don't be in a hurry. Take your time. Enjoy the process, not the goal. If you fall in love with the grind you will enjoy the long journey up your own personal mountain so much more.

I want leave you with this story from the book *Pound the Stone* by Joshua Medcalf. When a stone mason is trying to crack a large stone he pounds on it again and again with his trusty hammer. To the outsider looking at him, it would seem that he isn't getting anywhere. No matter how hard he hits the stone it doesn't budge.

He pounds that stone one hundred times and still nothing. But when he hits that stone again, it finally cracks. It wasn't this last hit that cracked the rock; it was all that pounding he did before. Without the first one hundred hits he would never have been able to crack that stone.

On your Filmtrepreneurial journey there will come times when you feel like you are pounding your own stone and nothing is happening. That you are wasting your time because you aren't seeing the results. This is the time where you have to put your head down and pound that stone. I promise you, if you keep at anything in life long enough, sooner or later you will crack that stone for yourself.

WANT TO BE A FILMTREPRENEUR?

Bring the Filmtrepreneur message to your organization, convention, university or film festival. We offer keynotes, on-site workshops, and seminars. Just visit www.filmtrepreneur.com/events.

Alex Ferrari also offers consulting and coaching services to guide you on your filmmaking or screenwriting journey. Just visit www.alexferrari.com.

To hire Alex to speak at your next event visit www.alexferrari.com/hirealex.

For more information on all the platforms and services IFH Industries has to offer visit the sites below.

– WEBSITES –

Filmtrepreneur: www.filmtrepreneur.com
Filmtrepreneur Podcast: www.filmbizpodcast.com
Filmtrepreneur YouTube: www.filmtrepreneur.tv

Indie Film Hustle: www.indiefilmhustle.com
IFH Podcast: www.indiefilmhustle.com/podcasts
IFH YouTube: www.indiefilmhustle.com/youtube
Indie Film Hustle TV (Streaming Service): www.ifhtv.com

Bulletproof Screenwriting: www.bulletproofscreenwriting.tv
BPS Podcast: www.screenwritingpodcast.com
BP Screenplay Coverage: www.covermyscreenplay.com

– WORKSHOPS –

Make Your Movie Bootcamp: www.mymbootcamp.com
The Filmtrepreneur Retreat: www.filmtrepreneur.com/retreat

– BOOKS –

Shooting for the Mob: www.shootingforthemob.com

– INDIE FILM HUSTLE FILMS –

On the Corner of Ego and Desire: www.egoanddesirefilm.com
This is Meg: www.indiefilmhustle.com/thisismeg

SPECIAL THANKS

To my beautiful wife, Maricruz Ferrari, for her undying love and support of my filmmaking ambitions. Without her, I would never have started *Indie Film Hustle* and, in turn, never have written this book.

To my children who inspire me to become a better man every day.

To Connie H. Deutsch, for not only being my book editor but for always being a supportive and loving guide throughout my journey.

To my Mom and Dad for their support of my crazy filmmaking dreams.

To every independent filmmaker who has ever crossed my path. You were the inspiration for this book. Thank you.

GLOSSARY OF TERMS

Ancillary Product: the creation of additional product lines that can spin off from a feature film, video content or television/streaming series.

AVOD (Ad-Supported-Video-On-Demand): refers to ad supported based video on demand and is typically free to the end user.

Cosplay: when fans dress up as a specific fictional or real-life character, usually at conventions or events

Crowdfunding: the practice of funding a project, via a crowdfunding platform online, by small amounts of money from a large group of people.

Crowdsourcing: the act of outsourcing tasks once only able to be done by employees to a larger crowd, generally over the Internet.

DCP (Digital Cinema Package): could be seen as the digital version of a 35mm film print. Its main advantage is that you can present it to theaters to enable them to project it via a digital projector.

Film Aggregators: act as a conduit between film distributors/filmmakers and online digital platforms like Netflix, Apple TV and Google.

Growth Hacking: a new field of marketing focused on the massive growth of start-up companies that have small budgets and a small amount of time. The term was made popular within the Silicon Valley business start-up community.

Hustle: the ability to never give up on your dream no matter what obstacle is placed on your path. To grind day in and day out until you achieve your life's mission.

IP (Intellectual Property): an intangible creation of the human intellect. In the film industry this usually comes in the form of copyrights and trademarks of characters, feature films, television shows or any video content.

OTT (Over-the-top): was first coined in reference to any device that would go "over" a cable box to give customers access to video content delivered over an Internet connection.

P&A (Prints and Advertising): the costs associated with marketing, advertising and the promoting of a feature film.

ROI (Return on Investment): the ratio between the profit and the cost of the film or product investment.

ROT (Return on Time): the ratio between the time you invest in a project or venture and the monetary returns of those actions

SVOD (Subscription-Video-On-Demand): is a video service that allows the customer to access an entire video library for a small recurring fee.

TVOD: (Transactional-Video-On-Demand): is when you rent or purchase a film to other video content outright on any platform.

Viral Marketing: is a marketing strategy that leverages existing social media networks to promote a product or service by consumers spreading and sharing information, in much the same way a virus spreads from person to person.

VOD (Video-On-Demand): is when customers are given the ability to consume television, movie or any video content whenever they choose.

ABOUT THE AUTHOR

Alex Ferrari is a best-selling author, blogger, speaker, consultant, the host of the #1 filmmaking podcast on iTunes *Indie Film Hustle Podcast*, and an award-winning writer/director with 25 years of experience in the film industry. As a director, his films have screened in close to 600 international film festivals. As a post-production professional Alex has collaborated with hundreds of filmmakers and delivered or worked on over a thousand projects including feature films, television, commercials, network promos, music videos and streaming series.

Frustrated that his fellow filmmakers were being "chewed up" by the film business, Alex decided to start *Indie Film Hustle®*, a website dedicated to educating filmmakers and artists on how to survive and thrive in the film business. He also launched a podcast focused on filmmaking called *The Indie Film Hustle® Podcast*. Within three months of its start date the show became the #1 filmmaking podcast on Apple Podcasts. He's also the host of the popular screenwriting podcast *Bulletproof Screenwriting®*, and the filmmaking business podcast *Filmtrepreneur®*.

After launching *Indie Film Hustle*, Alex created the world's first streaming service dedicated to filmmakers, screenwriters, content creators and artists called *Indie Film Hustle TV* (IFHTV). Alex has dedicated his life to helping people realize their dreams using IFH and IFHTV as platforms to do so.

Alex's feature film debut was the award-winning *This is Meg*. The film stars comic actress Jill-Michele Meleán (Reno 911, MadTV), along with Krista Allen, Joseph Reitman, Debra Wilson, Carlos Alazraqui, and Jenica Bergere. Alex wore many hats on this indie film including directing, producing, cinematographer, cameraman, editor, and colorist. The film was licensed to Hulu and is available on IFHTV, Apple TV, and Amazon.

Alex's latest project is the feature film *On the Corner of Ego and Desire*. A satirical look at the indie film world shot entirely at the Sundance Film Festival. The film world premiered at the Raindance Film Festival. His first book *Shooting for the Mob* (Based on the Incredible True Story) hit the Amazon Best Seller's List within a few weeks of its release.

Alex currently lives in Los Angeles with his lovely family. He is a devoted practitioner of meditation and how it aids in the creative process. He also speaks regularly at screenwriting and film events, festivals, schools, and conventions.

CPSIA information can be obtained
at www.ICGtesting.com
Printed in the USA
LVHW101130140323
741587LV00006B/702